W9-BVY-120

P E N T E C O S T 3

**INTERPRETING
THE LESSONS OF
THE CHURCH YEAR**

LUKE T. JOHNSON

**PROCLAMATION 5
SERIES A**

FORTRESS PRESS MINNEAPOLIS

PROCLAMATION 5
Interpreting the Lessons of the Church Year
Series A, Pentecost 3

Cover and interior design: Spangler Design Team

Library of Congress Cataloging-in-Publication Data
(Revised for vol. [5] thru [8])

Proclamation 5.

    Contents: ser. A. [1] Epiphany / Pheme Perkins —
[2] Holy week / Robert H. Smith — [etc.] — [8] Easter /
David Buttrick.
    1. Bible—Homiletical use.   2. Bible—Liturgical
lessons, English.
BS543.5.P765 1993   251   92-22973
    ISBN 0-8006-4177-9 (ser. A, Advent/Christmas)
    ISBN 0-8006-4178-7 (ser. A, Epiphany)
    ISBN 0-8006-4179-5 (ser. A, Lent)
    ISBN 0-8006-4180-9 (ser. A, Holy week)
    ISBN 0-8006-4181-7 (ser. A, Easter)
    ISBN 0-8006-4182-5 (ser. A, Pentecost 1)
    ISBN 0-8006-4183-3 (ser. A, Pentecost 2)
    ISBN 0-8006-4184-1 (ser. A, Pentecost 3)

Manufactured in the U.S.A.   AF 1-4184
97   96   95   94   93   1   2   3   4   5   6   7   8   9   10

CONTENTS

Introduction

Preaching from the lectionary catches us in some curious mental quandaries. As responsible preachers, we do not want to manipulate the Word of God but to place ourselves under that Word for its judgment and grace. It is probably because we have such convictions that we use the lectionary. We resist the sort of thematic preaching that picks texts as ornaments for a thesis, or as instruments for generating an emotional response from the hearers. We turn to the lectionary because we want to encounter the Word as Other. We figure the lectionary is as close to that encounter as we are likely to get on a regular basis. Yet when we open the lectionary we do not encounter the Word as truly Other. We meet God's Word not in a pure but in a packaged form. The lectionary itself represents the work of human hands. In its selections, its snippings, and its shapings, that work at times reveals the same manipulative instinct we distrust within our own hearts.

Nor is it obvious how we should approach these readings. Even considered separately, each lection forces on us a number of reading decisions. Should we receive it as a timeless oracle addressed directly to our hearts from God? Or should we read it within its original literary context? Already we are placed in a painful tension between openness and closure. When we return the passage to its first context, we can hope in some fashion to "close" its meaning. But if we allow it to float free from its literary moorings, then the text is open to any number of possible meanings.

The tension is increased when we consider two or three such texts placed in juxtaposition. Now we are invited not only to treat these passages as though they are wholes and not parts, but also as though they are naturally to be read in conjunction with these other texts from all over the Bible. The very structure of the lectionary asks us to struggle with these three (or more) texts as though God's Word is to be found in their arrangement. Fair enough. Yet any careful observer of the lectionary recognizes that the readings don't just fall together at random. The signs of human calculation are obvious. The Old Testament reading regularly presents a theme which is found again in the Gospel and perhaps more obliquely in the Epistle. The pattern of typology, or of prophecy/fulfillment suggested by this arrangement did not happen by accident.

The lectionary preacher is therefore caught in a dialectic between openness and closure, between the fragmentary and the whole. To avoid "closing" the Word in predetermined personal prejudices we open our minds and hearts to the presence of God's Word in the lectionary; yet the lectionary quickly reveals to us its own very human and prepackaged "closing" of biblical texts.

To make matters even more complicated, lectionary preaching takes place in the liturgy, which introduces a still further tension. The liturgy is at once real life and not real life. As ritual, it has a wholeness and a completeness that our fragmentary selves nowhere else achieve. Ritual allows us to make believe that we are in fact what we long to be: God's people, shaped by God's Word, a fellowship in the Spirit, the body of Christ. It encourages the fantasy that we live through a "liturgical year" of seasons shaped not by the cycles of nature or secular history but by the events of our "salvation history." The liturgy encompasses us with a mesh of meaning far denser than most of us experience in our daily lives.

Yet ritual is very much "real life" as well. For one thing, we never altogether lose the fragmentariness we bring to worship. We never meld totally into the action of the worship assembly. But the ritual is also "real life" in that it *does* for a moment make us something more than a collection of fragments, create of us something more than the sum of our disparate individual lives. Ritual allows us to cross "time zones" into the seasons of the church's liturgical year, to draw from that rich source the strength to live out our life's other moments. To borrow ancient sacramental language that is echoed by cultural anthropologists, ritual is a sign that effects what it signifies.

How interesting all of these factors make the task of preaching from the lectionary in the liturgical assembly! We come from fragmented lives to juggle fragments of texts, seeking both with texts and our lives to find some structure, some stability, some closure. Given the power of this natural urge to a fixed and definite meaning, some comforting and final resolution, all this complexity can seem a distraction not worth the effort. Perhaps at some level that is why many of us never take up, or quickly abandon, the lectionary.

But the mental and emotional strain we experience in preaching from the lectionary in the liturgical assembly mirrors and enacts the essential tension of our life of faith. We are creatures who constantly seek closure, not only in our reading and our thinking, but above all in our lives. We resent and resist God's call to openness and indeterminacy. We prefer the structures of our idolatries to the risk of obedient faith. At every moment we oscillate between obedience to the call of God that invites us into a wider and more perilous world of truth, and the choice of our narrower, form-fitted personal truths. None of us consistently at every moment lives out the response of faith. We may recognize that we are gifted and called by the One who moves before us. We may even step into the scary space of God's freedom. But no sooner do we get there than we start to furnish it with our usual bric-a-brac to make it comfortable.

Closure and openness: Such is the essential stress of faith. Our experience of it in the struggle to be faithful to these biblical texts—that is, to be open to the meaning to which God calls us, while feeling the pull toward an easy, comfortable, predictable lesson—is precisely the struggle of faith within the mind and heart of the preacher.

The great advantage of the lectionary read in the context of the liturgy is that it brings all the elements of this struggle of faith into explicit focus. The preacher struggles with the fragments of life and the fragments of texts within structures that invite premature closure, then seeks to *hear* the Word of God that may not be obvious within all the human words with which it is clothed. Does this seem terribly agonistic? So I conceive it, and so I experience it. And such is the shape of the reflections you are here invited to share.

Since I take seriously the struggle of faith both in life and in preaching, these reflections all have a certain dialectic character. I try to catch within the echo chamber of my own rhetoric some sense of the voice other than my own seeking expression in the human and therefore humbling exercise called preaching. The readings occur in the "off-season" of the liturgical year, on Sundays blandly designated as "ordinary time." The natural point of reference for our reflections is our ordinary life in the world. How do these texts challenge us to live in the humble circumstances of our daily lives with the nobility of those belonging to God's kingdom?

Twentieth Sunday after Pentecost

Lutheran	Roman Catholic	Episcopal	Common Lectionary
Isa. 5:1-7	Isa. 5:1-7	Isa. 5:1-7	Num. 27:12-23
Phil. 3:12-21	Phil. 4:6-9	Phil. 3:14-21	Phil. 3:12-21
Matt. 21:33-43	Matt. 21:33-43	Matt. 21:33-43	Matt. 21:33-43

CARING FOR THE VINEYARD OF THE LORD

I have suggested that a dialectic between openness and closure is inevitable in the struggle to preach faithfully from the lectionary. The readings for this Sunday quickly reveal it. The Old Testament reading from Isaiah is "answered" so deliberately and emphatically by Matthew that it is difficult not to accept the package offered. Indeed, so perfect is the typological joining between prophecy and Gospel that we almost forget to notice the reading from Philippians that does not seem to *fit* at all. Yet precisely that lack of fit will provide us the opportunity to establish a more vigorous and open conversation between these texts and our lives. The proper place to begin, however, is with the obvious closure. We can do this by considering the first sort of reading of prophet and the Gospel that the lectionary arrangement itself invites.

FIRST LESSON: ISAIAH 5:1-7
A FIRST LOOK AT ISAIAH

Isaiah's "Song of the Vineyard" may be so familiar to us because of its appropriation by the Gospels that we can fail to hear it clearly, and miss some of its nuances. We automatically take the side of the planter whose creation and care for a plot of ground made it to be a vineyard in the first place, and whose elaborate constructions of watchtower and vat made clear his legitimate expectation for a healthy harvest of grapes. We sympathize with his disappointment at the vineyard's failure to yield anything but wild grapes, and perhaps even understand his angry decision to let such an unfruitful plot of land return to wilderness. But should we not pause over the degree of the landowner's anger? He not only tears down the wall and removes the hedge, thereby leaving the vines vulnerable to predators; he not only refuses to prune the vines and allows them to be overrun with briers and thorns; he actually commands the clouds to give it no rain, so that it will be utterly destroyed: "I will make it a waste." Such emotion appears excessive, such actions extravagant when directed at a piece of earth.

Our sense of disproportion grows when, without warning, one of the characters in this "love song"—the "beloved" whose vineyard this is—suddenly and without warning addresses the hearers, demanding of the inhabitants of Jerusalem and the men of Judah a "judgment" between himself and his vineyard. We recognize in this personification that the "vineyard" is not simply a piece of ground but symbolizes a group of people. The song of the vineyard, even in its first setting, is thoroughly allegorical in character. The key to the allegory is supplied by the prophet himself: "The vineyard of the LORD of hosts is the house of Israel, and the people of Judah are his pleasant planting" (5:7).

We now know the characters and the relationship: The planter is the Lord God and the vineyard is God's people. The making of the vineyard is God's creation of this people from nothing; the elaborate accoutrement of the field is God's nurturing of this people. The owner's expectation of grapes and disappointment at the rank growth of "wild grapes" therefore must be . . . what? It must refer to an appropriate response of the people to the Lord who created and cared for them. The conclusion of the passage indicates what that appropriate response should have been: not the worship of God, not acts of religion, but rather moral behavior, the deeds of "justice" and "righteousness." The growth of wild grapes is also spelled out in terms of moral behavior among this people: rather than justice and righteousness, there is "bloodshed" and a "cry."

The song of the vineyard is therefore parabolic in character, pointing to the specifically *covenantal character* of the relationship between the Lord and Israel. The Lord has kept his side of the covenantal obligations by creating and nurturing them. But the people have failed by refusing to show the covenantal qualities of righteousness and justice in their relations with each other. Now we can understand the otherwise puzzling designation of the passage as a "love song," for—as we see also in Hosea, Jeremiah, and Ezekiel—the covenantal relationship is classically portrayed in the prophets in terms of the covenant of love between a man and a woman. And we grasp the reason why the singer refers to the creator of the vineyard as "my beloved," for the prophets were those in Israel who were the spokespersons for this covenantal relationship with the Lord.

We may thereby perceive as well why this parable—lifted from its context—lent itself to appropriation by the Synoptic Gospels and to its present lectionary arrangement. The Christian reader recognizes at once in the designation *beloved* a reference to the "beloved son" Jesus, and can therefore apply the story to Jesus' story, especially since the failure of the vineyard involved bloodshed, as did also the rejection of Jesus as Messiah. It was easy to fit the parable within another, a cognate, allegorical code.

But before turning to that appropriation of the passage, we ought to linger a moment longer over the perhaps puzzling choice of the vineyard as the metaphor for the covenantal relationship. Why the choice of an agricultural image to play out the expectation and failure of a moral response? To answer this, we need to return the passage for a moment to its original literary context. If we scan the sayings of Isaiah that precede the account of his call in chap. 6, we can observe three things: First, that the prophet's attacks on the people have as their consistent focus the connection between idolatry and social injustice; second, that this social injustice is spelled out mostly in terms of the covenantal commandments having to do with agriculture and property; third, that the image of the vineyard occurs earlier with reference to the fate of the people following upon their observance or nonobservance of these commandments. Because of the injustice in the land, the prophet says in 1:8, "daughter Zion is left like a booth in the vineyard, like a shelter in a cucumber field, like a besieged city." Even more impressively, the prophet attacks the "elders and princes" of the people for their oppression of the poor, saying, "It is you who have devoured the vineyard, the spoil of the poor is in your houses" (3:14). In contrast, the promise of the restoration that will follow upon the observance of the law is expressed in similar agricultural terms: "They shall beat their swords into plowshares, and their spears into pruning hooks" (2:4).

Isaiah's "Song of the Vineyard" provides full parabolic expression to this imagery, precisely at the point where the turn between blessing and curse is made explicit. The song is immediately preceded by a glowing image of Israel's restoration when the people ask to "be called by your name" and their reproach is taken away: "The fruit of the land shall be the pride and glory of the survivors of Israel" (4:2). But the song is followed by the most explicit series of condemnations of those who practice oppression of the poor. Notice how this is spelled out in terms of adding "house to house . . . field to field," with the result that there are so many houses that the vineyard has no more room, and "ten acres of vineyard shall yield but one bath, and a homer of seed shall yield a mere ephah" (5:8-10). Those who do this are characterized in terms of their gluttony and drunkenness (5:11), which in turn derive from the fact that they "do not regard the deeds of the LORD or see the work of his hands" (5:12).

My reason for looking at this Isaian passage so carefully is to begin loosening it from the typological closure that prevents us from seeing it fresh. As we turn now to the way in which the Gospel of Matthew takes over and transposes the Isaiah "Song of the Vineyard" as an allegory of the sending and rejection of God's beloved Son, we are aware that this appropriation does not exhaust the possibilities of meaning in the Isaiah passage, possibilities that remain open to us as well.

GOSPEL: MATTHEW 21:33-43
MATTHEW'S CREATIVE CLOSURE

That Jesus spoke a parable concerning a vineyard and its wicked tenants seems supported by its appearance both in the Synoptics and in the Gospel of Thomas 65. The exact shape of the parable as spoken by Jesus, and in particular the degree of self-referentiality it may have involved, are less clear because the sources provide different readings of the parable. The version Matthew has taken over from Mark 12:1-12, however, contains an explicit allusion to the Isaian "Song of the Vineyard" in these words: "and put a fence around it, dug a wine press in it, and built a watchtower," (v. 33) which are found in these two Gospels and Isa. 5:2, but not in The Gospel of Thomas 65 or in Luke 20:9.

At the very least, the inclusion of the Isaian words within Jesus' parable makes his words echo those of the prophet and creates an unmistakable example of the fulfillment of prophecy. And when this parable about a "beloved son" is placed in the context of controversy with the Jewish leaders who will then be termed responsible for Jesus' death ("bloodshed"), we see a new level of allegory at work. The Matthean version retains the image of the vineyard as the people Israel, but picks up the Isaian attack on "the elders and princes of his people" (Isa. 3:14) as the ones responsible for its failure to yield the fruit of righteousness desired by God. The Matthean parable thus becomes an allegory of the long history of God's relations with Israel as a series of failures to obey the "owner of the vineyard." The multiple sending of emissaries is clearly meant to refer to the sending of the prophets. The sending of the son equally clearly refers to Jesus, who is cast out of the vineyard and killed (21:39).

We notice that this appropriation of the Isaiah passage represents a closing of its meaning as well. The sort of righteousness demanded by God no longer involves all the ways in which relations between people are governed by covenant, but solely the reception of God's emissaries, the prophets. The failure of righteousness, likewise, is sealed by the rejection of God's final emissary, the son. Such narrowing of application affects the conclusion of the parable as well. The punishment is not, as in Isaiah, directed to the vineyard as such (being left desolate), but solely to the vinedressers who sought to gain the inheritance. The vineyard will be taken away from them and given to others who will "give him their fruits in their seasons" (21:41; RSV).

The specific application of the parable to Jesus' opponents is made emphatically clear by the closing citation from Ps. 118:22-23, "The stone that the builders rejected has become the cornerstone; this was the Lord's doing, and it is amazing in our eyes" (21:42). This passage from the Psalm figures in several New Testament discussions of the rejection of those who reject the Messiah (see Acts 4:11; 1 Pet. 2:4, 7). But notice that the logic of the parable and the logic of Matthew's narrative alike demand that those who are rejected should be precisely those leaders of the Jews who correspond to the vinedressers of the vineyard of the Lord. Indeed, Matthew himself concludes by noting, "When the chief priests and the Pharisees heard his parables, they realized that he was speaking about them" (v. 45). What could be clearer? Nevertheless, the broader context of *Jewish* rejection of the messianic preaching about Jesus has found its way into the passage. In Matthew's version alone we find placed in the mouth of Jesus himself: "Therefore I tell you, the kingdom of God will be taken away from you and given to a people [RSV: nation] that produces the fruits of the kingdom."

This is at once a frightening and generalizing closure. Not only is the parable referring specifically to the rejection of Jesus during his lifetime, but also to the refusal of the Jewish "nation" to accept the Christian preaching of Jesus as Messiah and Lord. Therefore, the text stands as a condemnation not only of those leaders of the past who had a role in Jesus' condemnation, and who therefore lost their role as leaders of the people (see 21:41 and Luke 20:16), but as well of the entire nation that has rejected the Christian proclamation, the Jewish people.

And since those Jewish members of the Sanhedrin are long gone and of no interest to us who now hear this reading in the lectionary, who are we most obviously to think of as the ones condemned? Exactly! The "unbelieving Jews" of every age who resist the Christian message. By "closing" the Isaian passage to a specific messianic reference, and then "opening" it to a perpetual application to all who reject the beloved son, the Gospel of Matthew has—perhaps inadvertently—created another and more dangerous sort of closure that is immediately evident to those of us who read it now in the lectionary.

What, after all, are the options given to us when we read in sequence the Isaiah passage and the Matthean parable? We are invited to see one parable as clarifying the other, and the first as fulfilled by the second. We are asked to see in the rejection of Jesus the logical conclusion of a long and tragic series of rejections of God by the Jews, resulting in their nation being rejected from the kingdom of God preached by Jesus and inhabited by Christians. Now we can either bemoan or celebrate this conclusion, but it is the one the arrangement of the texts invites. We can rejoice because we are now the Lord's vineyard and the Jews are not. We can use the text as a proof against the Jews that they had their chances but ruined them. And the passages have in fact so been read in the history of Christian interpretation and preaching.

But how can these texts still be God's word to us? Do they retain any prophetic challenge to our lives? Is the meaning of Isaiah and of the Gospel exclusively in the past? Does its reach into our lives extend only to a sense of smugness and superiority for those of us fortunate enough to be Christians? Does the liturgical reading of the text lead only to self-congratulation and anti-Semitism? Surely this is not where we should end. We cannot allow ourselves to be closed by this closure. But where can we turn to force open so powerful a lock on our imaginations?

HEARING THE PROPHETIC WORD

We start by making two shifts in our accustomed way of hearing these texts. Suppose we take Isaiah as speaking directly to *us*, which is of course the premise of our liturgical reading of the prophet in the first place. Isaiah addresses not simply the Jewish people of the past, therefore, but all those who seek to live the "kingdom life" and bring themselves under the judgment and grace of his words. The vineyard of the Lord can refer in this case not to the covenantal relationship between the Lord and his people on the land of Israel, but to the covenantal relationship between God and humanity on the planet Earth. When we make this shift, we find ourselves unexpectedly addressed as caretakers of creation. Now the laws from Torah that spelled out the covenantal obligations concerning property and possessions, justice and oppression, can be read as addressed directly to us in our stewardship of the earth.

The second shift is to hear Matthew's parable not simply as an allegory of the rejection of Jesus by the Jews of that time, but as a parable that challenges those to whom the kingdom has now been given. The owner of the vineyard still seeks the appropriate fruit in due season, seeks righteousness and justice in the kingdom. If the rejection of the son in the parable stands as the ultimate sign of the rejection of God's demands on humans, then perhaps we can turn the equation around: The rejection of God's covenantal demands on us now also means in effect the rejection of God's Son and the abandonment of our identity. If we make these adjustments, we may hear both Isaiah and Matthew in a more pressing and powerful fashion. If we are held accountable by God for our stewardship of creation, then the prophet's attack on those who "add house to house . . . field to field" may apply to us with frightening directness.

SECOND LESSON: PHILIPPIANS 3:12-21
THE PHILIPPIANS CONNECTION

(For Phil. 4:6-9, see the Twenty-first Sunday after Pentecost.)

That these adjustments in perspective are not arbitrary is suggested by our third lectionary reading. We began this reflection by noting that it appears to escape the typological pattern of the prophetic and Gospel readings, and that its lack of fit offers us the warrant for opening up the other texts. Paul encourages the Philippians to strive for progress in their transformation into the image of Christ (3:12-21). Such progress demands what he calls a "maturity" in understanding (3:15), which can come from imitating those who already exemplify the messianic paradigm in their lives (3:17). In this letter, Paul has presented to their consideration four such examples: Jesus the Messiah (2:5-11), Timothy (2:19-24), Epaphroditus (2:25-30), and Paul himself (3:2-11). What do the examples have in common? They demonstrate the proper response of faith as opposed to idolatry.

Faith in God receives life and identity as a gift, not as something to be grasped or accomplished. Idolatry, in contrast, seeks to seize life and worth by what we accomplish. The path of faith leads to a life of self-emptying service to others: We need not cling to life because it is ever renewed by gift of God. The path of idolatry, however, must be always self-seeking and possessive; nothing can be shared, for every loss is total. The way of idolatry is one of closing upon the self and every self-realization. The way of faith is a constant opening to the presence of God in the circumstances of our worldly lives. And this means that faith, unlike idolatry, can never stop, but must always "press on . . . straining forward to what lies ahead." The gift given Christians is not for their smug possession, but for their transformation into gift-givers in the world.

Why does Paul present just this understanding of maturity? Because even within the Philippian community, there are some who are competing with each other, showing party spirit and rivalry (1:15-17; 4:2-3). Paul knows that all such competition derives from the spirit of envy, and that envy is the attitude appropriate to idolatry. The Spirit given us by God, however, leads to the open sharing of all of life through fellowship (2:1-4). The purest expression of faith is the sharing of life with others, when each person looks not only to one's own interest but also to the interests of others (2:4). For Paul such faith can be summarized simply in the phrase, "the mind of Christ" (2:5). Christians find the classic expression of this "mind" in the hymn of Phil. 2:5-11, which shows the Messiah's obedience "to the point of death—even death on a cross" (2:8). The opposite example is found in those whose lives are dominated by self-seeking. They are quite literally "enemies of the cross of Christ" (3:18).

Paul makes this contrast between faith and idolatry explicit when he refers to those bound by the Spirit as having their "citizenship in heaven," and those who are enemies of the cross in these terms: "their end is destruction; their god is the belly; and their glory is in their shame; *their minds are set on earthly things*" (3:19). This language should remind us of Isaiah's. Paul has touched on the inner drive that causes humans to seek only their own pleasure, possessions, and power, to their ruin and that of others. Paul and Isaiah join in seeing the rejection of God's covenant in terms of such antisocial, self-aggrandizing, and hostile behavior. The difference is only that Paul sees the fulfillment of the covenant spelled out perfectly and emblematically in the obedient faith of Jesus, and the ability of humans to imitate that faith given by the Holy Spirit. But the call to this obedience is as constant to us now as to ancient Israel, and the terms are the same: God seeks from the vineyard justice and righteousness.

HEARING THE WORD

How have we "matured" in our understanding of what God demands of us over the past two thousand years? At one level, the basic drama has not changed: The human heart is drawn by the call of God but also is driven by idolatry. But we have begun to see that the demand placed on us for justice and righteousness is more inclusive than we might earlier have perceived. We have begun to see that the vineyard of the Lord is not simply the people Israel, nor is it simply our community or the church. God has placed us as responsible for the vineyard ✓ that is creation. We have come to that realization terribly slowly, and largely as a result of disaster.

We are at last beginning to perceive that our idolatrous impulses, spelled out in arrogant self-aggrandizement, envy, and greed, have led to the oppression of

13

the poor and the near-destruction of the planet. Because our "minds are set on earthly things" (as in Phil. 3:19) or because we "do not regard the deeds of the LORD or see the work of his hands" (as in Isa. 5:12), we persist in the senseless exploitation of natural resources, adding "house to house . . . field to field," for the extravagant privilege of the few (mostly First World people), and the oppression and destruction of the many (mostly Third World people).

It is not necessarily a cause for congratulation that we who have exploited the poor and the Earth in order to support a needlessly, heedlessly opulent style of life, have come to our senses not because God's Word has convicted us but because we are now in danger of eliminating the sources of our pleasure: our pillaging of the vineyard is at last making it "a wasteland." It is, we must admit, our fear and not our faith that has moved us at last to make the first small steps toward ecological consciousness. Is it an exaggeration to apply to us Paul's words, "their glory is in their shame"?

THE FRUIT OF THE VINE/
THE CUP OF BLESSING

Those of us who hear this word of judgment also share in the cup of blessing at the table of the Lord. And in the Eucharist, we enact an identity as a people that is not yet entirely achieved by any one of us individually. The ritual of the Lord's Supper draws together these texts and breathes into them the life of the Spirit and the breath of hope. For here we celebrate creation as the vineyard of the Lord when we raise the cup of wine and declare it in words of blessing to be the "fruit of the vine." And here we remember how the Lord Jesus poured out his life for all, so that as we share in his "cup of blessing" we hope also to share in his life-giving Spirit. We hope that as we join the mysteries of creation and covenant to that of our salvation through the death and resurrection of Jesus, our hearts might be transformed and our minds made to mature, so that our stewardship of the earth might begin with the recognition that all we are and have is fragile gift from God, to be received in thanksgiving and to be used as a blessing.

Twenty-first Sunday after Pentecost

Lutheran	Roman Catholic	Episcopal	Common Lectionary
Isa. 25:6-9	Isa. 25:6-10a	Isa. 25:1-9	Deut. 34:1-12
Phil. 4:4-13	Phil. 4:12-14, 19-20	Phil. 4:4-13	Phil. 4:1-9
Matt. 22:1-10	Matt. 22:1-14	Matt. 22:1-14	Matt. 22:1-14

QUALIFIED HOPE, PROVISIONAL REJOICING

As in the lectionary readings last Sunday, Matthew's Gospel once again picks up a vivid image from the prophet Isaiah. Now it is not the vineyard of the Lord, but a feast catered by the Lord. The Gospel parable once more turns the image into a symbol of rejection for Jesus' historical Jewish opponents. And once again, the reading from Philippians seems at best only loosely aligned with the other two.

These texts, however, do not fall into so obvious a typological pattern. The Matthean story of the marriage banquet, for example, is not a simple parable of rejection. Instead, it combines in complex and double-edged fashion both invitation and refusal, with reference not only to the Jews of Jesus' day, but to the readers of the Gospel in every age who also are called to respond to the invitation of God.

Each reading combines a statement about God's action with one about human response. Read together, the texts provide an occasion for reflecting on the character of God's call in our experience and in the responses we make. Our reflection can begin with the prophetic promise. At first it seems nothing but positive affirmation. Only slowly does it reveal the ambiguities implicit within it. As we observe in turn the way Matthew and Paul exploit different aspects of the prophetic text we search as well for the questions they put to us.

FIRST LESSON: ISAIAH 25:6-9
THE FEAST OF RICH FOOD

When Isaiah promises that the Lord will make a feast "on this mountain," he is renewing a still earlier pledge. Deuteronomy had spoken of the feasts of rejoicing that the people would enjoy in Jerusalem if they observed the commandments and statutes of the Lord. Such feasting would express God's blessing of the people for their fidelity to the covenant (Deut. 12:7, 12, 18).

The prophetic renewal of the promise, however, has a distinctive character. It follows a series of prophetic warnings and laments over the nations that surround and oppose Israel, bringing to the land not a blessing, but devastation. Babylon (13:1-22; 14:4-31), Moab (15:1—16:13), Damascus (17:1-14), Egypt (18:1—19:25), and Israel's coastal neighbors (20:1—23:18) are condemned. Israel itself is threatened with devastation because it has abandoned the covenant (17:7-14). But interspersed between these condemnations are words of comfort addressed to Israel (14:1-11, 32; 19:24; 22:20-25). The prophetic oracles eventually reach a cosmic scope: "The LORD is about to lay waste the earth . . . and scatter its inhabitants" (24:1-20). In the middle of such cosmic collapse, the Lord will reveal his power: "The LORD of hosts will reign on Mount Zion" (24:23).

The prophet transforms the terms of blessing and curse. The future feast is not a reward for the people's performance (it has not been impressive), but is based on God's fidelity. Both Israel and the nations will suffer the consequences of their refusal to acknowledge the Lord. The cause for celebration is that even during the time of devastation and loss, the Lord has remained "a refuge to the poor, a refuge to the needy in their distress" (Isa. 25:4). Despite the rejection of his demands by Israel and the nations, God has continued to provide the possibility of an "opening" for his people.

If this promised feast is grounded not in human accomplishment but in the work of God, it also takes on more than local or temporary significance. It extends to all nations, and has an eschatological dimension. Isaiah repeats that the feast is to be "for all peoples," and not simply for the Jews (25:6-7). Its joys celebrate more than the removal of hunger by a successful harvest; God will "swallow up death," and thereby relieve human life of its most tragic dimension: "The LORD God will wipe away the tears from all faces," not only for a space of time, but forever (25:8).

Consider the boldness of the prophetic word. His declaration follows upon the repeated condemnation of the people for failing the covenant, and the constant interpretation of the nation's disasters in terms of that apostasy. Yet rather than offer a diminished version of hope, the prophet actually elevates expectation by proclaiming a "feast of rich food" that surpasses any possible temporal realization. Such expectation can be based only in the power of God.

In the second part of the Isaiah passage, the people make a double recognition of the One who caters this feast: "This is our God . . . this is the LORD." They also twice declare, "We have waited . . . we have waited." Why have they waited? "That he might save us." And now that the Lord has brought the feast there is the response, "Let us be glad and rejoice in his salvation" (25:9). This response suggests another and still another dimension of the eschatological feast.

We see that salvation here means more than a good crop or escape from invaders; it means the removal of death and the causes of sorrow. We recognize further that not humans but only God can accomplish this work. And now we detect that the feast somehow consists in the very presence of the Lord. The people proclaim, "We have waited for *him* . . . we have waited for *him*."

The magnificent vision is all the more stirring because it addresses circumstances that appear so unfavorable. But the prophetic word also contains ambiguities. The feast is promised for all peoples, yet it is to take place, as the prophet twice affirms, on this mountain, indicating Jerusalem. Is the eschatological reversal of the human condition, then, to be restricted to one place on earth?

And what does the prophet mean by "the shroud that is cast over all peoples, the sheet [RSV: veil] that is spread over all nations?" The Hebrew is obscure, and only the context makes us think of it as a veil of mourning. The prophet says that the Lord will "destroy" this veil. But why was it there in the first place? Why was it over the nations and not over Israel? And why does the climax of the promise concern not all the nations but specifically with Israel: "The disgrace of his people he will take away from all the earth" (25:8)?

The prophet's promise vacillates between a feast open for all that consists in a fundamental healing of the human condition because of the presence of God, and a promise that is temporally realized for the benefit of the elect people of the covenant. Within the context of the prophetic text, it is the local, temporal dimension that prevails, for this saying is followed immediately by the promise that as "the hand of the LORD will rest on this mountain," it will also crush Israel's neighbor Moab (Isa. 25:10-12). Nevertheless, the Isaian text contains startling elements of universality and ultimacy that offer themselves to new circumstances and further interpretation, all the more so since both the feast and the rejoicing are yet promise only: "The LORD of hosts *will* make . . . it *will* be said on that day."

GOSPEL: MATTHEW 22:1-14
A DISASTROUS WEDDING PARTY

Matthew's parable of the wedding banquet (Matt. 22:1-14) finds approximate parallels in the versions given by Luke 14:16-24 and The Gnostic Gospel of Thomas 64. But Matthew's version is distinctive, in the way it shapes the parable itself, in its addition of a coda, and in its placement. To start with the last point, we notice that Matthew places the parable immediately after that of the vineyard (see pp. 9–11), and addresses it to the same audience of Jewish leaders. We therefore expect it to have much the same point. The expectation is enhanced when we observe that the marriage banquet is given by a king "for his son" (22:2; compare 21:37-38), so that we are virtually invited to identify *this* son also as "the beloved one" Jesus, sent by God to the people and rejected by them, and to read the parable as pointing to Jesus' ministry.

The structure of Matthew's version also points that way. Note the contrast to Luke 14:16-24. Luke lacks any specification concerning the man who "gave a great banquet." Matthew speaks of a "king" providing for his "son" what is repeatedly termed a "wedding banquet" (22:2, 4, 8, 9). These elements suggest multiple connections to the biblical imaging of covenantal relationships in terms of marriage, and to the Isaian promise of an eschatological feast of rich food. In contrast to the two-fold invitation in Luke's version, furthermore, Matthew has a series of three invitations. This feature also reminds us of his parable of the vineyard. The resemblance is made still clearer when we observe that the king first sends "slaves" and then "other slaves," and that these meet not only a refusal of the king's invitation but seizure, shameful treatment, and murder (22:6; see Matt. 21:34-36). Finally, Matthew has the king respond to such violent rejection with equally fierce revenge: He "was enraged. He sent his troops and destroyed those murderers, and burned their city" (22:7). He extends the invitation to others only after the removal of those first invited. In this way too, the parable matches the conclusion of the parable of the Vineyard, and suggests a direct identification of this punishment with the destruction of the city of Jerusalem.

Following Matthew only this far, we can read the parable in strictly typological fashion. Isaiah had foretold God's preparation of a feast for the people. But they continually refused God's invitations, ending with a violent murder of God's prophets. As a result, they themselves are removed and others invited to the feast. Read this way, the story celebrates the rejection of the Jews and the invitation of the Gentiles to the feast of God's kingdom. It is, in every sense of the word, a parable of closure.

But that would be to stop before Matthew himself stops. Matthew adds a coda to his parable that subverts its first obvious closure (22:11-14). The king encounters a wedding guest without a wedding garment or an answer to the king's query as to how he got in without one. The king thereupon has the guest thrown "into the outer darkness" (22:13). What are we to make of this strange addition, so signally absent from the Gospels of Luke and Thomas? The language suggests the work of the evangelist, especially the statement about being thrown into the darkness where there is weeping and gnashing of teeth (compare Matt. 8:12; 13:42, 50; 24:51; 25:30). Matthew works Jesus' parable into a stark tale of rejection by and of the Jewish people, but then extends it to a further and even more pointed threat of rejection. Those who have been called and have accepted the invitation may still be rejected from the feast!

Puzzling over the meaning of the wedding garment does not get us very far. Was it given to guests as they came in? Would any guest be expected to have one? Was the king unfair to ask someone taken from the street to have the appropriate clothing? We don't really need to invoke the cultural background. The structure of the parable is clear enough if we resist reading Luke's version into Matthew's. In Luke, there is an emphasis on people being compelled to enter, and that these included "the poor, the crippled, the blind, and the lame" (Luke 14:21-23). Matthew has neither emphasis. People are simply invited—not forced—from streets and thoroughfares, with no mention made of their economic or social condition. There is every reason to think that the wearing of a wedding garment was within their means. And since the guest has no answer to the king's question, we can assume that the question was fair and the guest was at fault.

The wedding garment must be connected to the characterization Matthew himself gives to the invited guests: They are "both good and bad" (22:10). The failure to wear a wedding garment signifies the failure to behave according to the standards of the kingdom that the wedding banquet symbolizes. Here is a pervasive Matthean theme found in other parables addressed to the disciples. As in the parables of the weeds of the field (13:36-43), the nets and fishes (13:47-50) and the sheep and goats (25:31-46), there is a division made between the good and the bad—even within the members of the kingdom itself. Each of these parables also has the same refrain as this one: Those who are rejected are thrown "into the outer darkness, where there will be weeping and gnashing of teeth." The church is not made up simply of the sanctified. It contains people "both good and bad." The church, therefore, is not yet the eschatological wedding banquet, but a place and time of testing. As Matthew's conclusion makes plain, "Many are called, but few are chosen" (22:14).

Matthew seems to lock Jesus' parable into the past: The Jewish people rejected the sending of God's son, and the Gentiles were invited in. But then he decisively turns the past visitation into a challenge for his own church: They are the Gentiles who have been called into the wedding. They are a mixed assemblage of good and bad. Now is their time of testing. Are they appropriately dressed or not? Do their deeds correspond to the righteousness demanded of the kingdom to which they have been invited? Do *they* at least recognize the seriousness of the situation in which they find themselves?

The Gentiles should not too quickly appropriate to themselves the Isaian promise concerning the feast of rich food, that the veil covering the nations would be removed, and that every tear would be taken away. Matthew reminds those invited that the full realization of the promise is ahead, and there is still the chance to choose the wrong garment and to be cast into the place of weeping.

SECOND LESSON: PHILIPPIANS 4:4-13
A MOVEABLE FEAST

The Philippians passage echoes the motifs of rejoicing and of waiting for the Lord (4:4) found in Isa. 25:6-9. But it speaks more directly and satisfyingly to the situation of those who read these texts today, because it locates the true source of our rejoicing and the character of our waiting. From Isaiah we gain a vision of a future feast, whose eschatological dimensions strain against the limits of a single place or a single nation and seek realization in the presence of God to all peoples. From Matthew we receive warning that others before us missed calls to the feast, and that our invitation to the marriage (given by our initiation into the church) is not yet the final celebration; there is still a time of testing. Paul brings us home to the everyday world of our life together.

Paul reminds us (we appropriate to ourselves the titles of "brothers and sisters" in the text) of the richness of our present lives "in Christ Jesus" (Phil. 4:7). We are not yet in the end time. We too are among those who wait. But our waiting for the Lord is fundamentally changed because of the gift of God's presence already given in Jesus. Now our awareness that "the Lord is near" means not simply that the end is temporally near, but that God's presence is always pressing upon us.

Paul suggests that the feast of God's presence is a moveable one. Even the circumstances associated with absence and deprivation can be turned to positive effect. Waiting makes us irritable when it is empty. But because we wait in the presence of the One who is coming, we can make our "gentleness be known to everyone" (4:5). We can live simply and sweetly rather than in a barely controlled rage. Waiting can also lead to anxiety if its outcome is not certain. But because we wait in full confidence in the one who has already gifted us, we can in fact be free from anxiety (4:6)—or at least at some level!

Because of the gift of the Holy Spirit mediated to us by the resurrection of Jesus, our time before the end is not empty but full, not lonely but gifted with presence, not powerless but powerful. Paul declares that "I can do all things through him who strengthens me" (4:13). His statement should not of course be taken beyond its intent: The *all things* refers to doing the things needful for our life together in this in-between time, and I do them not under my own steam, but by the empowerment that comes from the Lord. Thus the essential element in Paul's confidence is found in prayer. It is in "prayer and supplication with thanksgiving" that the empowerment to live in the presence of the One whom we still await is mediated. Prayer anticipates and realizes the very presence for which we long. It is already a participation in the feast, and therefore the reason why Paul can so enthusiastically enjoin the attitudes appropriate to a festival: "Rejoice in the Lord always; again I will say, Rejoice" (4:4)!

Paul does not by any means suggest, however, that this sense of God's presence (which is the very essence of the feast whose fulfillment we await) is automatic or simply to be assumed. That would be like showing up at a marriage banquet without a wedding garment. Appropriate attitudes and behavior are required. So Paul recommends to the Philippians that in addition to their prayer, in which "the peace of God" will guard their minds and hearts in Christ (4:7), they should live out what "you have learned and received and heard and seen in me" (4:9). As in the lectionary passage from Philippians last week (3:17-21), Paul tries to provide his readers with an example of how to live out "the same mind" as Christ (2:5). His somewhat florid listing of the things they are to "think about" is similarly evocative of the qualities found in Phil. 2:1-4, now translated into the language of virtue: "whatever is true, whatever is honorable, whatever is just, whatever is pure, whatever is pleasing, whatever is commendable, if there is any excellence, and if there is anything worthy of praise" (4:8). Such attitudes and behavior not only make "the peace of God" available to them, but—in a stunning phrase reversal—"the God of peace will be with you" (4:9).

Paul acknowledges in fact that the Philippians have demonstrated such qualities in their concern for him (4:10). He is making reference to the gift of money sent him by the Philippians (4:16). The Philippians have provided a feast for Paul by their care. So he can now also "rejoice in the Lord greatly" (4:10). In the Christian community, the gifts of care and concern and mercy and forgiveness and mutual strengthening themselves enact the presence of the Lord.

Paul's own attitude toward their gesture is critical. If he does receive the gift as a mediation of God's presence then he cannot but "rejoice in the Lord." And Paul does recognize and does rejoice, because he has learned "to be content" (4:11). The Greek term used by Paul (*autarkēs*) evokes the rich tradition of Greek philosophy with its ideal of self-sufficiency. Its appearance here is in fact surprising, for we associate the stern ideal of self-sufficiency less with a community of feeling and mutual caring than with a life apart. But Paul employs the term precisely in this context of mutuality. He says that he has learned how to live in all kinds of circumstances and not to complain of want. He is able to do this because for whatever is truly required he is enabled by "him who strengthens me" (4:13). Because we are gifted by God we are freed from the anxiety that forces us to cling to our lives, and are enabled to be content. And we can thereby recognize in gifts from others, however small and ordinary and everyday, the feast catered by God for our rejoicing.

We confess that the liturgical assembly—and above all the Eucharist—is an anticipation of the eschatological banquet to which we have been invited by our baptism, and in which the presence of the Lord is mediated to us not only in the humble gifts of bread and wine but also in the spiritual availability that we bring each to the other. Is it not the failure to wear the appropriate garment when we so lack "contentment" that we refuse to open ourselves to that presence, when we (in our attitudes and gestures) say to each other that we would rather be at the farm or at the business (Matt. 22:5)? Is this not to "make light of" the invitation of the Lord (Matt 22:5)? By withholding our presence from each other (in mind and heart if not in body) do we not withdraw also from the presence of the Lord?

Twenty-second Sunday after Pentecost

Lutheran	Roman Catholic	Episcopal	Common Lectionary
Isa. 45:1-7	Isa. 45:1, 4-6	Isa. 45:1-7	Ruth 1:1-19a
1 Thess. 1:1-5a	1 Thess. 1:1-5a	1 Thess. 1:1-10	1 Thess. 1:1-10
Matt. 22:15-21	Matt. 22:15-21	Matt. 22:15-22	Matt. 22:15-22

FAITH SEES WHAT CANNOT BE SEEN

The lectionary sometimes presents us with a set of texts so locked into obvious alignment that to breathe the fresh air of God's word and not the stale and accustomed air of our own preconceptions we must push and shove against that arrangement. The opposite also happens. Sometimes the lectionary texts appear to have fallen together haphazardly. When this happens, we are more easily aroused to the challenge of discerning within an apparent incompatibility some subtle signs of affinity. So today: Deutero-Isaiah's proclamation concerning the servant of the Lord seems to have little connection with the confrontation between Jesus and the Pharisees concerning payment of taxes to Caesar, and still less to Paul's thanksgiving for the way the Thessalonians had first heard the gospel. But a faithful attempt to see what is not obvious here may lead us also to see something about faith itself: that it sees what cannot be seen.

FIRST LESSON: ISAIAH 45:1-7
WHOSE WORK IS THIS?

The prophecy from Isaiah is remarkable in its calling the Persian king Cyrus the Great the one "anointed" by the Lord, "whose right hand I have grasped." Not only does this locate the prophetic word in the world of ancient politics, but it does so in a decidedly odd way. The historical setting for the oracle is the Babylonian exile. Jews carried off from Jerusalem by Nebuchadnezzer had been rallied by the Second Isaiah to a sense of expectation for a return to the land accomplished by God (Isa. 40:3-11; 41:8-20, 25-28; 42:16-17; 43:8-21; 44:1-5, 24-27). The promises have been high in fervor, but low in specific content. The rhetorical weight of these affirmations runs the risk, in the face of nonfulfillment, of increasing incredulity and even despair. The gap between expectation and realization, between the word of the Lord and concrete human experience, grows dangerously great.

Now the Persian king Cyrus has taken power (ca. 550 B.C.E.), threatens the Babylonian empire, and conquers it in 539 B.C.E. Will the exile now come to an end? Shortly after conquering the Babylonian empire, Cyrus will in fact issue the edict enabling the Jewish exiles to return to the land of promise. Such a rapid turnabout presents a problem to the prophetic interpreter. On the one hand, what the prophet promised is about to happen. That's the good news. On the other hand, the fulfillment appears to be happening not as a direct result of Yahweh's intervention, but by the workings of human warfare and statecraft. For a prophet, that's news of a more dubious character.

Deutero-Isaiah sees something that others (perhaps even he) had not at first seen. If Yahweh is not just a tribal deity but the only true God, the ultimate source of all that is, then Yahweh is the source also of this historical turn. The Lord is not just the battler for Israel against its foes, but governs all the universe. This implies that not only Jewish leaders are Yahweh's agents, but also the leaders of other nations. The prophet's faith in Yahweh enabled him to see beneath a politician's success a more profound truth concerning God's rule: It extends over all peoples, and can use all of creation to accomplish its ends.

With daring, Deutero-Isaiah turns in the passage immediately before this one to the Persian king and addresses him in the voice of "the LORD who made all things" (44:24): "'He is my shepherd, and he shall carry out all my purpose'; and who says of Jerusalem, 'It shall be rebuilt,' and of the temple, 'Your foundation shall be laid'" (44:28). If a foreign king can accomplish the purposes of the Lord in building the city and restoring the temple, then he deserves the traditional titles of Israel's leaders. Cyrus can appropriately be called the Lord's "shepherd," and even, "his anointed."

Consider more closely the implications of the prophet's perception. First, God's action in the world is not to be found only in separate "sacred" events, but in all the moments of human existence. The presence of God is not to be found where nothing else is present, but rather the opposite: Anything that exists points to the presence of God. God works in and through human instruments, both in this prophet who now speaks and in this king who now conquers. To "see the work of the Lord," is not necessarily to see something different from what others see, but to see the same thing differently.

The second implication is that Yahweh's power extends beyond his people Israel to all the world, a perception that contributes to the development of radical monotheism: one ultimate power is the source of all reality. If Yahweh can raise up a foreign king to do his bidding, then he is truly Master of the universe. Thus, this passage concludes, "I am the LORD, and there is no other. I form light and create darkness, I make weal and create woe; I the LORD do all these things" (45:7).

So radical is Isaiah's vision that it is susceptible to distortion. The first distortion is to so quickly universalize God's work that one forgets that the Master of history plays a deep game not accessible to easy analysis. Isaiah is far from saying that God works equally and indiscriminately in all circumstances; rather he states that there is purposefulness beneath the apparently random events of history. In this case, Isaiah asserts that the choice of Cyrus is made by "the God of Israel" for his own purposes, namely "for the sake of my servant Jacob, and Israel my chosen." Cyrus is not even aware that he is an instrument in God's hands: "I surname you, though you do not know me" (45:4). "I arm you though you do not know me" (45:5). It is not because he is aware of the Lord or seeks any goals except his own that Cyrus is chosen—any more than Israel was chosen as servant because of its goodness and fidelity. Cyrus has his role to play in God's plan, and so does Israel. Their roles are not their own choices. Indeed, they do not even know their lines until they are given them to be spoken. They do not themselves know how the drama will turn out. We meet here again the scandal of particularity. If God can work through any and all human instruments, why are these the instruments chosen?

A second distortion could identify any great display of power with the divine, and any overwhelming human agency as God. And since in earthly terms no human being exercises so much effective power as an emperor, it is easy to attribute divinity to the king. This is the distortion called idolatry. It involves less a theoretical than a practical apprehension of the world. If God is ultimate power, whatever I choose to treat as ultimate is effectively God for me.

Deutero-Isaiah is therefore concerned to make clear that Cyrus' conquest of other nations derives from Yahweh's power rather than his own. It is because Yahweh has taken him by the hand (45:1) that he is able to accomplish these things. Isaiah addresses Cyrus himself, so that the reminder of whose power is at work becomes an invitation to the Persian king to conclude from what he has accomplished that Yahweh is the Lord: "I will give you the treasures of darkness and riches in secret places, so that you may know that it is I, the LORD" (45:3).

In reality, of course, the prophet addresses his own people, who could be swayed by Cyrus' display of power into thinking that they owed their freedom to him and thereby give him the homage owed only the Lord God. So Isaiah makes clear his own purpose, "that they may know, from the rising of the sun and from the west, that there is no one besides me; I am the LORD, and there is no other" (45:6).

GOSPEL: MATTHEW 22:15-22
WHOSE COIN IS THIS?

If we interpret Deutero-Isaiah's prophetic vision as a "seeing of what cannot be seen" in history, a seeing that demands a discrimination between the manifest powers that seduce us to idolatry and the implicit power that summons us to faith, then we better appreciate the choice of the Matthean passage to be Isaiah's lectionary partner.

The story of Jesus' confrontation with Jewish leaders concerning payment of taxes to Caesar is found in all three Synoptics. Matthew has only lightly modified the version he found in Mark. In contrast to Luke 20:20, for example, he has maintained the distinctive "political" character of the confrontation by retaining the identification of Jesus' challengers as "Pharisees and *Herodians*" (22:16). We are not sure who the Herodians (= "partisans of Herod") were, but their presence with the Pharisees places us in the context of first-century Palestinian politics. A brief summary of that context helps clarify the intent of the question concerning taxes to Caesar, and the point of Jesus' response.

Jews in Palestine were deeply divided over the issue of how to align religious loyalties and social institutions. Their divisions were generated by the challenge to Jewish identity posed by the cultural hegemony of Hellenism and the political suzerainty of Rome. How much could a Jew engage Greek culture and still be a loyal child of the covenant? How far could a Jew cooperate with Roman authority? The issues had sharper definition in Palestine than in the diaspora, for in *eretz Israel* it was more difficult to separate symbols from institutions. One could not simply spiritualize the temple worship; one had to choose whether to make sacrifice at that place or not. Jews divided among themselves according to these decisions. At one end of the spectrum were the Sadducees, who found it possible to combine their Jewishness with a strongly positive view toward Greek culture and a co-operative attitude toward Rome. At the other extreme, Essenes and Zealots both actively resisted Greek ways and Roman rule, and refused to recognize as Jewish anyone who *did* associate with them!

The question put to Jesus was therefore not a theoretical proposition concerning the relation of church and state. It was a litmus test concerning his identity as a Jew, and by implication, his loyalty to the Lord as Master of history. The opponents suggest the incompatibility of God's rule with Roman occupation: A loyal Jew must renounce the idolatrous government of Rome! To heighten the tension, the question is put publicly in Jerusalem, in the precincts of the temple at the time of Passover. This was a place and time at which hundreds of thousands of Jews gathered in the city for the pilgrimage feasts, often in a frenzied mood of religious patriotism and rebellion. Matthew notes that Jesus perceived the "malice" in the question, whereas Luke notes its "craftiness." Both are accurate. First the craftiness: The one who has been proclaiming the kingdom of God seems forced to choose between the rule of God and human power. Flattery is employed— the disciples of the Pharisees begin by noting that Jesus "shows[s] deference to no one." Also the malice: By being forced to respond to an inflammatory test in those circumstances, Jesus ran the risk either of being rejected and stoned by his fellow Jews (if the tribute was approved) or of being executed by the Romans as a fomenter of revolution (if the tax was disapproved).

Jesus' statement that they should give to God "the things that are God's" and to Caesar "the things that are Caesar's" is neither evasive or sophistical. Neither does it neatly divide parts of the world governed respectively by God and any human rule. Rather, it states in prophetic fashion the absolute incommensurability of the two kingdoms and the nature of the obedience they require. The obedience demanded by God goes far beyond anything required by any state, because God is the source of all that is: "The earth is the Lord's and the fullness thereof" (Ps. 42:1). All of reality is responsible to God. As Jesus will shortly declare, we owe to God the allegiance of our heart, all our soul, all our mind (Matt. 22:37). But such allegiance can neither be adequately measured nor impeded by any human rule or ordinance.

Jesus' opponents imply that recognizing the image or inscription of Caesar means idolatry and an abandonment of covenant with the Lord. But Jesus resists that easy equation. To give back to Caesar his own coinage is simply to recognize a fact of political life, not to abandon the rule of God in our hearts. Jesus' capacity to make this distinction is in fact given unconscious expression by these opponents themselves when they describe him as showing deference to no one (22:16). The translation of the Greek is not exactly accurate, for the phrase echoes those descriptions in Torah of righteous judges who do not judge by appearances, but judge fairly according to truth.

The opponents use this description to flatter and manipulate Jesus. He is not supposed to recognize the persons of the Romans! But he is not bribed by their flattery or their pressure. Instead, he accuses them in turn of hypocrisy. There are four progressively deeper ways in which the charge is true. First, although they praise Jesus for being no respecter of persons they are in fact trying to force him to judge by appearances, by making an expedient or foolhardy decision based on the inscription and image on a coin. Second, they themselves collude in the system of "idolatry" that is the Roman taxation by having a coin available to present to Jesus. If they were truly separate from Roman ways they would not use the coins. There is no fundamental difference between using coins for commerce and paying them in taxes. Third, they are hypocrites above all because by trying to force a choice between loyalty to God and obedience to Rome, they have reduced God's rule to a single possibility: It can only be manifested in the reign of a Jewish king. Fourth, their malicious question puts the lie to their recognition of Jesus as one who is "sincere and teach[es] the way of God in accordance with truth"; if they really thought that, they would not have sought to "entrap him in what he said," but would have sought from him teaching on the kingdom of God.

Jesus' response recapitulates Isaiah's prophecy with unparalleled crispness: Since God is Master of the universe, God can work through whatever means he chooses, even the Roman empire. But faith demands of us the ability to see what cannot be seen. Even the mighty power of Rome is in the hands of the one God "who makes light and darkness, weal and woe" (Isa. 45:7). To give back to Caesar what is his cannot therefore take anything away from God. First because everything Caesar "has" also comes from God, and second, because what God asks of us, the total devotion of heart, soul, and mind, has never belonged to Caesar and cannot be given back to him. Whose coin is this? Caesar's. Let him have it. Whose heart and mind and soul are yours? God's. Give them back by thanksgiving in every circumstance.

SECOND LESSON: 1 THESSALONIANS 1:1-10
WHOSE WORD IS THIS?

Paul's prayer of thanksgiving for the first Christians in Thessalonica appears at first to have little to do with the first two readings. However, the same quality of faith described by the prophet and the Gospel is spelled out here in terms most familiar to those of us who now seek God and must see what cannot be seen in the circumstances of our worldly lives.

This letter was written (in all probability) only a short time after the tumultuous founding of that community. As described in Acts 17:1-9, that beginning was anything but auspicious. Paul's preaching in the synagogue drew from the Jews some few converts to Messianism and more from God-fearing Greeks. Even this limited success created resistance among the other synagogue Jews, leading to a riot, an assault, an arrest, and a disturbance in the city so profound that Paul had to be taken away to Beroea quietly by night. There was nothing in any of this that could have been perceived as unequivocally the work of God. The founding of the church in Thessalonica, in fact, seemed all too obviously entangled in the ambitions and jealousies of humans.

Nevertheless, Paul's language declares that he sees something in the events of weeks previous that were not apparent. His thanksgiving (as it continues past our lectionary passage) makes reference to the external realities when it acknowledges that they had received the word "in spite of persecution" (1:6). But everything else in Paul's prayer focuses on realities no outsider could have perceived. This small group of adherents is "God's assembly" (*ekklesia*, 1:1), and a part of the "elect/chosen people" (*ekloge*, 1:4), characterized by the "work of faith and labor of love and steadfastness of hope" in the Lord Jesus Christ (1:3). More daringly still, he declares that the good news he had preached to them came "not in word only, but also in power and in the Holy Spirit and in full conviction" (1:5).

Is Paul's language simply a theological fantasy woven around the ambiguous circumstances of that community's beginning? No, it is a different perception of the same events! When Paul refers to "the power" and "the Holy Spirit" that accompanied his first preaching, he is not invoking the working of spectacular miracles, but rather the power inherent in the message he proclaimed. What is the empirical evidence for that power? The fact that the Thessalonians themselves were brought to belief by it! They were not confused by the riot of charges and countercharges that followed Paul's preaching leading to his inglorious departure. They saw "what kind of persons we proved to be among you for your sake" (1:5) and became "imitators of us and of the Lord" (1:6). Their faith, hope, and love, were themselves the expression of the Holy Spirit and power and full conviction. Paul expresses it most clearly in the next chapter when he returns to these same events, "when you received the word of God that you heard from us, you accepted it not as a human word but as what it really is, God's word, which is also at work in you believers" (2:13).

In terms much closer to our own ordinary lives, we find the exchange of trust and commitment between Paul and the Thessalonians demonstrating the principles enunciated by the prophet and the Gospel. First, God can work through surprising and unexpected human agents to accomplish his plans: Cyrus can be God's anointed. Second, faith distinguishes the appearance and the source of power: Cyrus is not God but empowered by God.

It would have been easy for the Thessalonians to regard Paul simply as a fanatic and someone to be despised. Indeed, most of the Jews of that city did so regard him, finding nothing convincing in his scriptural demonstrations that the crucified Jesus was the Messiah (Acts 17:2-3). It would have been easy to join the popular riot against Paul and return to their accustomed ways. But they saw what could not be seen. They saw in a crucified criminal the fulfillment of their Scriptures. They heard in Paul's speeches the word of God. They were able to see in this unexpected and unlikely visitor to their city the agent of God's work.

Equally easy for Paul would have been to measure this unexpected success as due to his own ability and to claim for himself the Thessalonian's allegiance. But he sees in fact what they see. Their ability to perceive in his human speech the word of God was due to God's Spirit. Therefore the glory must be given to God, not to the preacher. He and his fellow workers do not preen, but "give thanks to God for all of you and mention you in our prayers" (1:2).

SEEING WHAT CANNOT BE SEEN

In three different ways, these lectionary readings invite us to reflect over the odd character of faith, hears voices others do not hear and sees visions others do not see. But unlike schizophrenia, faith makes visions real. Cyrus was not obviously the instrument of God, but because Isaiah was given to see him as such, so he became. Paul was not obviously the bringer of God's word, but because the Holy Spirit enabled the Thessalonians to see him as such, so he became. Jesus was not the obvious interpreter of God's rule, but because we have received his Holy Spirit, so we can perceive him, and so he is for us.

Similarly, none of us is obviously the bearer of grace to another. Assembled all in a heap liturgically, we are even less attractive as the embodiment of gift. But what should happen if we were to see each other as bearers of grace? Would we then reciprocally become such? What if we should see the liturgical assembly *itself* as a gift for each to receive? Would it then become such? The precedents are impressive.

Twenty-third Sunday after Pentecost

Lutheran	Roman Catholic	Episcopal	Common Lectionary
Lev. 19:1-2, 15-18	Exod. 22:20-26	Exod. 22:21-27	Ruth 2:1-13
1 Thess. 1:5b-10	1 Thess. 1:5b-10	1 Thess. 2:1-8	1 Thess. 2:1-8
Matt. 22:34-40	Matt. 22:34-40	Matt. 22:34-46	Matt. 22:34-46

WHAT DOES FAITH DEMAND?

The three texts for this Sunday have an obvious point of resemblance. All three contain statements of commitment to the one God. Exodus threatens destruction for anyone who sacrifices to another God than Yahweh (Exod. 22:20); Jesus responds to the question about the "great commandment in the law" with the declaration of wholehearted love of "the Lord your God" (Matt. 22:37); Paul recalls the initial conversion of the Thessalonian church when they "turned to God from idols, to serve a living and true God" (1 Thess. 1:9).

Less obvious are the ways the remaining material in the three passages might also be related. Why do the readings say the things they do in connection with monotheistic faith? This question about the texts of Scripture leads us in turn to ask about the full dimensions of faith in the living God, and in particular about the ethical dimension of that faith that distinguishes it from mere belief.

FIRST LESSON: EXODUS 22:20-26
IDOLATRY, FAITH, AND POSSESSIONS

The short section of commandments from Exodus follows the giving of the Decalogue to Moses. One injunction follows another without any apparent ordering principle. Some of the commandments take the form of cases, as in 22:25-26: "If such and such happens, such and such will follow." Other commandments, such as 22:21-22, have the more apodictic form of the Decalogue: "you shall (not)." Commandments concerning relations between members of the people, furthermore, mingle indiscriminately with directives concerning relations between the people and God. Thus, in our passage we find that sacrificing to another God other than the Lord will lead to being "utterly destroyed [RSV]," followed by specific instructions concerning the use of possessions (22:21-27), followed in turn by still another directive concerning the relationship with God: "You shall not revile God" (22:28).

Most striking in this arrangement—or lack thereof—is the implicit message it communicates: First, that all these commandments are of equal importance; and second, that relations with God cannot be separated from relations between humans. God takes both relationships with the same seriousness. The point is reinforced by the penalties attached to each offense. If sacrifice to another God leads to being utterly destroyed, the oppression of the stranger, orphan, or widow leads to the same result: "I will kill you with the sword" (22:24).

If there is any difference, it lies in the greater emphasis on offenses against other people, especially the defenseless. The Lord emphasizes his personal involvement with such cases: The Lord will "surely heed their cry" (22:23), and again, "I will listen" (22:28), and will respond, "for I am compassionate" (22:27). We see also that the retribution towards those guilty of such oppression is even greater than that leveled at those who sacrifice to other gods. Not only shall the offender be destroyed, but "your wives shall become widows and your children orphans" (22:24); they shall become prey to the same sort of predators.

This passage expresses the essential link found everywhere in Torah between covenant and social justice, idolatry and social oppression. The connection is made repeatedly in the law: Faith in the Lord demands justice and the sharing of possessions with the needy. The betrayal of the neighbor and the oppression of the poor is the direct expression of the abandonment of covenant. The prophets repeat the same refrain: Their attacks on idolatry focus on the social injustice they see as idolatry's inevitable corollary. The wisdom writings make the same connection. Clearly, there is an implied equation here that goes far beyond a mechanical arrangement of commandments. We are invited to ask, therefore, about the nature of a connection that seems so obvious to the biblical writers but so often escapes us.

One basis for the connection is Israel's primordial experience of the Lord grounding the covenantal relationship with him. The Lord had created them as a people by taking them from their condition of slavery in Egypt and "doing justice for them" against their oppressors. The Lord has thereby identified himself as a God on the side of the oppressed. Therefore a fundamental element of the covenant is that as the Lord has acted toward this people, so must they act toward each other. They are to remember that they were once themselves "aliens in the land of Egypt" (22:21) and exercise toward the dispossessed among them, the sojourners, widows, and orphans, the same compassion and care as shown to themselves. To be in covenant with *this* God, therefore, means to obey all the directives forbidding oppression and commanding the sharing of possessions with those in need. To worship other gods means, in the same equation, to disobey those same commandments and practice injustice or oppression with regard to property and possessions.

There is a still deeper basis for the connection between faith in the one God and the covenantal commands concerning the righteous use of possessions. The Lord, after all, is more than a tribal deity and the covenant is more than an arrangement with a local suzerain. Israel confessed that the Lord who had brought them out of Egypt was the creator of heaven and earth. He was the source of being for all creatures. At a deeper level, faith in Yahweh therefore means to recognize God as the giver of existence itself and then of all other things. Yahweh gifts all equally with everything that is necessary to them. Humans are not in competition for existence or worth, but equally receivers of gifts. Their possessions can neither add nor detract from their being or their value. They can therefore generously share their possessions with each other.

In contrast, idolatry begins with the refusal to recognize our existence as coming from God and the search of being and worth in accomplishment. It therefore requires constant effort, a constant accumulation of the "having" that is the sole assurance of our "being." The idol of self-sufficiency will without such constant maintenance "die," for it has no life of its own beyond what is given it. The logic of idolatry equates being with having. Since there is only a limited amount of having available, the only way to be "more" is to make someone else "less," even if it requires stealing, fraud, and oppression. The combination of the Lord and of justice signifies something other than the accidental arrangement of legal materials. It reflects a dominant theme in Israel's self-understanding. The compassion showed Israel in its poverty must be reflected in Israel's compassion to the needy. It also explicates an even more profound theological conviction. Radical monotheism sees all being and worth as a gift from the one God demanding the sharing of possessions with each other.

GOSPEL: MATTHEW 22:34-46
LOVE OF GOD/LOVE OF NEIGHBOR

The Gospel reading is set in a series of scholastic controversies between Jesus and Jewish leaders in the temple preceding his arrest. Each of the Synoptics has a version of the controversy (Matt. 22:34-40; Mark 12:28-34; Luke 10:25-28). Luke is the most distinctive: He sets the encounter in Jesus' journey to the city, collapses the two commandments into one, and appends a parabolic response to the lawyer's casuistic challenge concerning the identity of the neighbor (Luke 10:29-37). Mark makes the interlocutor a scribe. Ordinarily Mark treats that group as Jesus' primary opposition. But in this case the scribe's response to Jesus with an approving recapitulation of the twofold law of love shows him to be "not far from the kingdom" (Mark 12:34).

Matthew has the shortest and crispest version. As we would expect from a Gospel whose structure and symbolism is shaped by controversy over claims to represent the authentic form of Judaism, Jesus is confronted by the Pharisees after they heard that he had "silenced the Sadducees," the school that before the destruction of the temple in 70 C.E. was their chief rival. One of the Pharisees, "a lawyer," asks a question that is meant to test him: "Which commandment in the Law is the greatest" (22:36)?

The question is similar to the one about paying taxes to Caesar, intended to place Jesus in an untenable position. Although there is some evidence from Jewish writings that efforts were made to compress the many laws of Torah into a smaller number of commandments or even a single principle, the relationship between Jesus and the Pharisees in Matthew's Gospel suggests that something more than academic curiosity was afoot. Jesus is being tested as a "teacher" (22:36) within Judaism in the hope that by misplacing the "great" commandment he might be identified as a deviant teacher and be discredited.

The summation of Torah by means of the Decalogue and Leviticus 19 is witnessed elsewhere in Jewish writings. So also is the isolation of respective duties to God and neighbor as representing the essential principles of obedience to God. But nothing prevents us from considering this particular formulation as deriving from Jesus. That Jesus in fact made a declaration combining the commandment to love God in Deut. 6:5 with the commandment of Lev. 19:18 to love the neighbor as the self seems probable, given the prominent place given to the law of love in other New Testament writings (see John 15:12; Gal. 5:14; Rom. 13:8-10; James 2:8).

A remarkable feature of Matthew's version of this encounter is that it has no proper narrative conclusion, not even a response from Jesus' questioners. Matthew's abrupt ending with Jesus' words shows that the evangelist is less interested in the historical conversation between Jesus and his opponents—or even in the way this encounter helped generate opposition to Jesus that led to his death—than in the authoritative character of Jesus' declaration. Whatever the Pharisees of the past or present might think of Jesus' summation, it represents for the Matthean church the authoritative teaching of the risen Lord, whose words mediate his presence among them until the end of the ages (Matt. 28:20).

We who now read Jesus' words in the liturgy hear them in the same way. We therefore turn from asking historical questions about the text to allowing the text to ask questions of our own histories. When the text is addressed to our lives, it is inappropriate to oversimplify or generalize its import, as though Jesus were saying "all you need is love!" Jesus' declaration in fact makes a clear distinction between the First and the Second Commandments. The First has priority in order but also in principle. It is identified as "the greatest and first commandment" (22:38). The second is "like" it in an essential way, but neither replaces nor adequately defines it.

The commandment of love toward God is total and open-ended. If one loves the Lord with *all* one's heart, and *all* one's soul, and *all* one's mind, then there is no end to it so long as there is life. Just as God is the source from which we draw our every breath, so must every breath be returned to God in acknowledgement, thanksgiving, and obedience.

The Second Commandment, however, contains a limitation. In the first place, no single "neighbor" can be the total recipient of my love; instead, many and different kinds of neighbors compete for my attention and compassion. In the second place, the qualifier "as yourself" places an obvious condition on the love for neighbor: It must be relative in character rather than absolute, just as my love for myself must be relative rather than absolute.

Despite these elements of dissimilarity, Jesus joins the two commandments. They are linked in terms of their essential character. Whatever love might mean, it applies both to God and to neighbor. And what love means here must be defined not in terms of our own preoccupations, but in terms of the covenantal context in which these commands were first given. The quality of *hesed* ("loving kindness") was with *emeth* ("fidelity"), the essential attitude demanded by covenant. They defined the appropriate dispositions toward the covenant partner. As the Lord showed *hesed we emeth* ("loving-kindness and fidelity") to the people, so were they expected to show the same qualities toward the Lord.

But how can such attitudes be demonstrated toward God? God is not explicitly nor palpably available to us. Instead, God is that hidden, implicit presence that deepens every "other" we do encounter in our lives, because God continually creates and sustains *everything* in existence at every moment. The way in which we encounter the others who are our neighbors in the world is therefore a means by which we can encounter the Other who is God. Thus the unity of response to God and neighbor. The differences are not collapsed. God is never simply identified with the neighbor. Our neighbor is certainly never to be identified with God! Nevertheless our keeping covenant with each other in loving-kindness and fidelity is the way God himself has chosen to enable our response to him with faith and love.

Perhaps all of us are willing to go that far, but the final part of Jesus' declaration also demands close attention: "On these two commandments hang all the law and the prophets" (22:40). This statement makes love of God and neighbor the organizing principle for reading all of Scripture. From this, Christians properly concluded that they were free from the customary regulations dealing in diet and ritual that did not fall under those principles. Of equal importance, however, Jesus' declaration also *maintains* the law and prophets as significant expressions of the dual commandment of love. It would be mischievous to interpret Jesus' declaration as though it contained only a purely formal principle to be filled any which way. By giving scriptural expression to these principles, Jesus points back to the demands of covenant as articulated in Torah and by the prophets.

In this way, Jesus' statement echoes the first reading. Jesus' words do not repeat the language about sacrifice to Yahweh (Exod. 22:20), nor the phrasing of lending money to one of God's people who is poor (Exod. 22:25), but they assert the inextricable link between genuine faith in the living God and the doing of justice with possessions. Taking Jesus' words seriously means uniting our devotion to God with the doing of social justice, and joining our commitment to social justice to our love of God, for each one depends on the other.

SECOND LESSON: 1 THESSALONIANS 1:5b-10
TURN TO THE LIVING GOD

Paul's recollection of the Thessalonian church's founding is appropriately placed within his epistolary thanksgiving: "We always give thanks to God for all of you and mention you in our prayers" (1:2). It is appropriate, because the entire theme of his recollection is the way their lives were given over to the power of God: They had received the good news "in power and in the Holy Spirit and with full conviction" (1:5). It is due to God's gift that they exist as church. Paul calls their response a fundamental "turning," or conversion: "how you turned to God from idols, to serve a living and true God" (1:9).

Paul uses the language of covenant derived from the law and the prophets. Human freedom must choose between competing claims to service. Humans can choose to obey powers promising the satisfaction of human craving for possessions, pleasure, or power. Doing so, they can maintain the illusion of independence from their Creator—a destructive illusion. The promising powers are sham, are only the projections of desire in the first place, and are kept alive only by the artificial resuscitation offered by constant human care. Idolatry is the pattern of compulsion centered on things that are not ultimate but are treated as such. Idols cannot provide any real life, for they have none of their own to share.

Humans can also choose to turn to God, the Creator of heaven and earth and all that is in them. This choice for life will not be disappointed. In contrast to the idols who stand only propped up by our devotion, the Creator is the living God who shares life freely and without grudging, by gift.

Paul further describes the Thessalonian conversion to the good news they had received. Their life is not only gifted by God with life and breath, but also by the grace of "the Lord Jesus Christ" (1:1), so that they now have "steadfastness of hope in our Lord Jesus Christ" (1:3). They have been "chosen" (1:4) for a covenant that builds on the covenants of creation and of Torah but transcends them. Through the Holy Spirit they have been gifted by a power for life that provides a hope for life beyond death. The kerygmatic statement of 1:10 continues: "to wait for his Son from heaven . . . Jesus, who rescues us from the wrath that is coming."

What is the basis for this expectation? The resurrection of the crucified Messiah from the dead to a new and powerful life shared with God: We "wait for his Son from heaven, *whom he raised from the dead*" (1:10). Only the "living God" can give life beyond the grave that is better and more powerful than that of the first creation. Thus we see the full conviction of the Thessalonians that accompanies and even enables their turning: The power of the Holy Spirit transforming them comes not from themselves but from the proclamation of a crucified Messiah. He is therefore alive and powerfully present among them! And if the crucified Messiah is now Lord, then the God who raised him is indeed the living God and the guarantor of their hope!

Paul asserts the centrality of faith in God. But does he retain the corollary of faith found in Torah and the gospel, namely covenantal attitudes and actions toward the neighbor? Paul develops this side of the equation in 1 Thess. 4:1-12. In subtle ways, however, it is found even in our lectionary passage. Notice how intricately the Thessalonians' "turning to the living God" is connected to their actions toward humans, first in their reception of Paul and his associates: "what kind of welcome we had among you" (1:9). The Thessalonians received the message "not as a human word but as what it really is, God's word, which is also at work in you believers" (2:13). Their hospitality toward the preachers, in other words, expressed and articulated their faith in God.

But they not only heard and believed. They also became "imitators of us and of the Lord" (1:6), with the result that they in turn became "an example to all the believers in Macedonia and Achaia" (1:7). The manner in which their faith was translated into a pattern of life according to the model of Jesus and of their apostles became a service to the faith of others: "The word of the Lord has sounded forth from you . . . your faith in God has become known" (1:8). Their example is so powerful that Paul declares "we have no need to speak about it" (1:8)!

WHAT DOES FAITH DEMAND?

Christian spirituality has tended to veer between an emphasis on faith and love of God so exclusive that it neglects the requirements of social justice, and an emphasis on love of neighbor so intense that it swallows any distinctive "love of the Lord" not identified with social action. Exclusive attention to either of these linked commandments leads paradoxically to the distortion and ultimately the nonfulfillment of the very commandment chosen. In the twofold covenant between God and humans, we show faith and love toward the God whom we do not see only by the care and compassion we show toward the neighbor we can see; likewise, we can only truly love our neighbors when they are regarded not as competitors for the scarce resources of being and worth, but as equal sharers in the gifts given by God.

In the liturgical assembly we gather to acknowledge God as our Creator and to give God thanks. But we do so as a covenant people. If we so focus on our private devotion to the Lord that we neglect (or grow irritated at) our neighbor in this assembly, we cannot love the Lord as he commanded us. But if we celebrate simply our presence to each other, we miss perhaps something even more important, namely that together we are all at every moment sharing in the same gift of existence, the same gift of grace, the same hope of eternal life, in the presence of the power that sustains us.

Twenty-fourth Sunday after Pentecost

Lutheran	Roman Catholic	Episcopal	Common Lectionary
Amos 5:18-24	Mal. 1:14b—2:2b, 8-10	Mic. 3:5-12	Ruth 4:7-17
1 Thess. 4:13-14	1 Thess. 2:7b-9, 13	1 Thess. 2:9-13, 17-20	1 Thess. 2:9-13, 17-20
Matt. 25:1-13	Matt. 23:1-12	Matt. 23:1-12	Matt. 23:1-12

THE INSIDER GAME

Passages of Scripture can have a powerful effect on shaping our identity, especially when we hear them in the liturgical assembly as "the Word of God." We are convinced that the identity thus shaped is positive. But even texts that build our identity positively in one way can also encourage (even if indirectly) far less attractive aspects of character. The texts read this Sunday have such a double-edged quality. Each contains a polemical attack on "outsiders" that encourages in the readers a sense of being "insiders" superior to those being attacked.

To be more accurate, the passages contain such polemic only in their unexpurgated version. Lectionary editors have deleted from the Pauline passage what they apparently regard as offensive material. I will treat the passage with the problematic material in 2:14-16 included. The readings challenge the way we as Christian readers play the insider game: the way we are tempted to, and the way we are called to.

FIRST LESSON: MICAH 3:5-12
PERVERSITY OF PROPHETS

The prophet Micah was an advocate for Yahweh during the tumultuous years of the late eighth and early seventh centuries B.C.E., when the Israelite monarchy sought to preserve itself against the encroachments of aggressive empires, and when professional prophets of the royal court provided official religious legitimation for political choices. Micah stood with Isaiah as a voice of independent judgment. He insisted that the covenant with Yahweh was not to be identified with national survival. Rather it contained a commitment and a promise that exceeded the safety of state institutions.

The passage read today (3:5-12) is a classic example of polemic between opposing charismatic figures. Micah attacks those he considers to be false prophets and the royal patrons who are eager for their words of reassurance. The prophet identifies in turn the objects of his attack, the reasons for his charges, and the judgment that will befall his targets. In the center of the polemic (2:8) is Micah's claim to represent the genuine voice of prophecy from the Lord.

Micah's most obvious targets are his professional rivals, termed the "prophets" (3:5) and "seers" and "diviners" (3:7), as well as "priests" (3:11). The terms suggest religious charismatics able to predict the future by means of visions or auditions. Micah can scarcely attack the possibility of such powers in principle, since he claims himself to have them (3:8). Instead, he addresses the perversion of their practices. His opponents are prophets for pay. They are not simply part of the salaried bureaucracy, they will also provide the desired prophecy for their fee: Their prophecies are given in response to a "bribe" or "money" or "price" (3:11). If the money is right, they will predict peace; but if payment is lacking, they will envision war (3:5). In a word, they are "leading [God's] people astray" (3:5) because they have made themselves into political instruments rather than spokespersons for the Lord. Their betrayal is the more profound because of the authority they have corrupted: They bring the "word of God" to bear on situations of national crisis without having listened for the voice of God, only for the jingle offered by the highest bidder.

Micah threatens such prophets with punishment. They will experience only darkness and not light. They will receive no more visions (3:6). They will have no answer from the Lord. They will end up in disgrace and shame (3:7). The form of retribution. It flows directly from their practice. The artist who paints only to the customer's taste loses the ability to see; the musician who plays only the crowd's favorite tunes loses the capacity to hear. Turning a gift into profit is a perilous proposition, for it risks the distortion and loss of the gift itself.

Micah equally attacks those whose bribes corrupt the prophets. They are the "rulers of the house of Jacob" and "chiefs of the house of Israel" (3:9). Their perversion of the prophets is consistent with the oppression they themselves practice (see 3:1-4). They are rulers who hate justice, prevent equity, and lead the people into bloodshed (3:9). In some sense, their condition is even more pitiable than that of the false prophets whom they bribe. They actually believe the messages they have thus purchased, telling themselves "Surely the Lord is with us!" (3:11). Such willful self-deception leads to a miserable end, described as the devastation of Jerusalem itself. The place where the Lord was truly supposed to be in the midst of them will be ruined: Zion will become a planted field, Jerusalem a heap of ruins, the temple mount a forest "because of you" (3:12).

Micah presents his own credentials in contrast to his rivals. He claims to have qualities that they lack: He is full of power, the spirit of the Lord, justice, and might. These qualities are not empirically demonstrable. But they enable him to deliver a message that is *not* likely to be desired, much less purchased by the court. He denounces the rulers' "transgression" of the covenant and their "sin" against the Lord (3:8) found in their efforts to camouflage their policies of oppression with the perversion of the prophetic spirit! In effect, Micah locates the integrity of his prophetic office in his refusal to be bribed into popularity and his willingness to risk the disapproval of the mighty. Only in such defiance of corruption can one be certain that the word comes truly from the Lord.

Against the professional seers who claim to be insiders to the power of the court, Micah claims another and superior "insider" status, that of the prophet of Yahweh. The controversy happened so long ago, and those of us who read it now so automatically assume the correctness of Micah's position and also our identification with it, that we may forget what a breathtaking and dangerous claim he is making. What keeps Micah (and us) from an even more appalling sort of corruption than that practiced by the rulers and their sycophantic seers? Is not the claim to be an insider with the Lord liable to an even greater perversion than prophecy-for-profit?

Indeed it is. The only thing to prevent the corruption that is smugness, self-satisfaction, and specious security is the awareness that the terms of polemic turned on the outsiders must be turned on Micah as well. The more open his attack on the outsiders, the clearer the standards defining his own practice. Now he must be held to his stance of independence and integrity! Now he is inviting everyone to measure him by the same standards by which he has measured others! The moment he ceases proclaiming "transgression and sin" in accordance with the demands of the covenant with Yahweh, that moment he becomes liable to the charge he has levelled against others.

The first and historical function of polemic, therefore, was to discredit opponents and show who is truly the insider. The more important function of this ancient polemic for the communities that have preserved it in their scriptures is to challenge insiders to meet the same standards of integrity defined by their attack on others.

GOSPEL: MATTHEW 23:1-12
THE HYPOCRISY OF TEACHERS

(For Matt. 25:1-13, see the Twenty-fifth Sunday after Pentecost.)

Micah's polemic against false prophets no longer embarrasses us because we all identify with the "right side." But this polemical passage from Matt. 23:1-12 is an acute embarrassment for many Christian preachers. The snippet chosen for the lectionary actually omits many of the harshest charges made against the scribes and Pharisees by Jesus. Enough remain to remind us of the rest. The scribes and Pharisees do not practice what they preach (23:3); they impose heavy burdens on others but do nothing to help in the carrying of them (23:4); their righteousness is one of show (23:5); they are hungry for prestige and adulation (23:6-7).

The reason for the hesitation to read such passages in the assembly is obvious. Characterizations such as these fed the stream of anti-Semitism that polluted so much Christian history, leading to the horrific events of the Holocaust. As Christians struggle to overcome their heritage of slander and hatred by means of multiple interfaith dialogues with Jews, it seems self-contradictory to continue to use such passages.

Even preachers who do not accept the contemporary opinion that the New Testament and Christology itself are intrinsically anti-Semitic are unwilling to read passages such as this. Sometimes the option of censorship is used. If the lectionary does not itself omit the reading, the preacher quietly replaces the offending sections with something more positive in character. But censorship places us in the position of judging what we want to hear from the Scripture, which is inherently corrupting, never ending, and self-defeating. If we do not read problematic passages in public and expose them to the light of preaching, attempting to create a healthy understanding of them, we simply turn them over to the far more dangerous realm of private and idiosyncratic interpretation. Failure to preach on hard texts is a betrayal of the preacher's responsibility both to the word and to the people.

The strategy of historical correction is not much better. It insists that Jesus was heir to the long prophetic tradition, and as a prophet within Judaism he was allowed to speak harshly to his fellow children of the covenant. This position argues that Jesus was not condemning all Jews but only a group of elite teachers, and that it was a misreading for Christians to take these attacks and apply them to every generation of Jews. These are important contextualizations. They should be respected as efforts to avoid the closure represented by a typological pattern directing readers to deduce that just as Micah battled the false prophets and they were judged by God, so were the false Jews condemned by the prophet Jesus and by God. They are therefore now outsiders to God's plan, and we who follow Jesus are the insiders. Any historical correction that helps remove that massive and idolatrous assumption is welcome.

Historical revisionism becomes self-defeating, however, when it paints first-century Jews in terms so positive as to deprive them of their humanity and the Gospel narratives of intelligibility. Contextualization also distorts if it moves from the legitimate observation that the form of the polemic in Matthew's Gospel derives in great part from the Christian encounter with Pharisaism in the decades after Jesus' death, to the illegitimate conclusion that the early Christians had abandoned Jesus' own perceptions by adopting anti-Semitism. Such conclusions are not really excessive; they do not go nearly far enough.

The historical reality is that Judaism was a deeply divided phenomenon during the time when Christianity was born. The school made up of Pharisees and their scribal allies on one side, and the school of the messianists on the other, were by the time of Matthew's Gospel simply the remaining combatants in a debate that before the fall of the temple in 70 C.E. had other lively voices. The debate concerned the proper way to be Jewish. The terms of the debate were often harsh.

It was common in the rhetoric of the period to charge opponents with the things Jesus here attributes to the Pharisees, and indeed far worse charges were flung between rival philosophical camps. At stake in the debate was the right to claim that one represented the authentic form of Judaism. The Matthean church therefore organized and shaped the traditions of Jesus' attacks on his opponents in light of its own continuing conflict with the emerging rabbinic tradition. It is an accident of history that the other voices to the debate have fallen away, leaving the harsh denunciation in Matthew's Gospel sounding isolated.

The polemical material in the Gospel is a legitimate and deeply human part of our tradition. Its capacity for harm derives from our misuse of the text. One way we can misuse it is to apply these denunciations to those it was never meant to address, namely the Jews of any succeeding age, as an instrument of our inexcusable anti-Semitism. But another way to misuse the text is to stop reading it simply at the denunciation of the outsiders. At least half of this passage addresses itself to the disciples of Jesus and therefore all those who read Matthew's Gospel in the church. Matthew deliberately and explicitly uses the polemic against the scribes and Pharisees as a foil for the positive instruction of the messianic community in 23:8-12.

The *literary* function of the polemic in Matthew's Gospel is therefore clear: The denunciation of the negative qualities demonstrated by the rival teachers who are outsiders is meant not to reassure but rather to challenge those teachers who are insiders. Jesus does not congratulate his followers because they are not like the others. His exhortation suggests that these disciples are all too willing to follow their example! And the attitude that they apparently find most tempting is the arrogance and elitism that Jesus most vigorously denounces in his opponents.

These Christian teachers too, we learn, are eager to be called "rabbi," and to receive the title "father," and to be termed "instructor." They must be called sharply back to the realization that in this community all are equal, all have one Father and one Master, who is the Messiah. They must be reminded of the essential lesson taught by that Master, the lesson of service even to the point of losing one's life: "The greatest among you will be your servant. All who exalt themselves will be humbled, and all who humble themselves will be exalted" (23:11-12). As arrogance and self-exaltation are condemned in the outsiders, even more so must they be among insiders as well.

SECOND LESSON: 1 THESSALONIANS 2:9-20
THE PERSECUTORS OF THE CHURCH

In this last reading, the lectionary editors have exercised the option of censorship to remove what they regard as an offensively polemical statement by Paul. What are their grounds for so mutilating the reading? Some scholars have recently argued that 1 Thess. 2:14-16 is a non-Pauline interpolation. In other words, it is not an original part of the letter deriving from Paul, but an addition fitted here by some later editor. Since there are no text-critical grounds for such an assertion, scholars have appealed to stylistic criteria: The vocabulary seems out of joint, or the length of the sentences appears arhythmic. In fact, such arguments have little weight, and serve mainly to expose the main reason for seeking to excise the passage, namely that it sounds embarrassingly anti-Semitic. The motivation is made even more obvious when we remember that the principle of authorship does not determine either canonicity or the value of a writing for the church. Do we refuse to read Colossians because its Pauline authorship is challenged? If the editors of this lectionary have omitted this passage, it is because they regard it as morally offensive or politically insensitive. In the present climate, they conclude, it ought not to be read to the people.

I sketched earlier my basic objections to the option of censorship: It reflects the arrogant assumption that we are in a position to determine what we should hear in God's word and what we can safely ignore; it is never ending, for there are always further sensitivities to appease; and, it is futile, for the removal of a text from the public realm only renders it more dangerous in the private realm. To exercise the option of censorship arbitrarily and under cover of committee, I submit, is an even more dubious and dangerous enterprise. Lectionaries are subject enough to manipulation simply in the matter of arranging materials. If the passages themselves are then reshaped to better fit our predilections, a more pernicious form of manipulation is taking place.

In the present case, the omission of Paul's statement concerning outsiders is particularly unfortunate. It distorts what remains of the Thessalonian passage by removing it from its literary context and from its historical plausibility. The Thessalonian passage is thereby robbed of its internal coherence. It is reduced to a set of bland affirmations without any context. The omission of materials also eliminates from the passage precisely the *dialectic* between insider and outsider that is present in the other two passages and that enables creative preaching to take place.

If we retain 2:14-16, we are able to read the rest of the 1 Thessalonians passage in a richer and more responsible fashion. As in the readings from Micah and Matthew, the negative portrayal of the outsiders functions as a foil for the positive portrayal of the insiders. It does so first in the case of the preachers. Despite facing the resistance from those Jews who "drove us out" and were "hindering us from speaking to the Gentiles so that they may be saved" (2:15-16), Paul and his associates have conducted themselves among the Thessalonians in a manner associated with love rather than anger or malice. For example, they worked with their hands so as not to impose a financial burden; they exhorted the population as a father would his children, providing encouragement as well as challenge; they presented an example of being "pure, upright, and blameless" in behavior "toward you believers" (2:9-12). They were, in short, the sort of teachers desired by the discourse of Matthew 23.

If Paul's behavior was not affected by his experience of persecution, then why does he bring it up? Partly because it is an important element in his understanding of his ministry: The rejection of the message concerning the crucified Messiah is intrinsically connected to the rejection of Jesus himself and of the prophets who preceded him (2:15). In this sense, Paul's invocation of a tradition of prophet-rejection functions as a legitimation for his ministry. But it is also an important element in his exhortation to the Thessalonians: Such suffering is also their inevitable destiny in a world that resists the truth. Thus it is an inevitable component of their reception of the gospel that they experience suffering. In fact, they have already—in the things they are experiencing at the hands of their "compatriots"—become imitators of the churches in Judea that had experienced rejection from the Jews (2:14).

The point here really is not the condemnation of the Jews of the past or even of Paul's present; indeed, he sees God as already effecting whatever retribution is due their rejection (2:16). The point is the perennial possibility of rejection by a hostile world for those who are dedicated to God's truth. Paul's characterization of this as "Satan block[ing] our way" (2:18) simply gives this reality its clearest statement. The fate of the prophets, the rejection of Jesus, the persecution of Paul, the suffering of the Thessalonians all are part of a tradition of witnessing to truth before a world that does not want to hear it.

And this enables us to understand, finally, why Paul is so eager to see this community again (2:17), and why he can speak of them so glowingly as his "crown of boasting before our Lord Jesus at his coming" (2:19). It is because they were able to *hear* the message Paul and his associates brought from God, and accept it, despite the threat and reality of persecution that accompanied it: "When you received the word of God that you heard from us, you accepted it not as a human word but as what it really is, God's Word, which is also at work in you believers" (2:13). They were willing to become outsiders to their own society in order to become insiders with God.

THE INSIDER GAME

It is fashionable in sophisticated circles to eschew the status of insider, even to one's own tradition. And the claim to be an insider certainly has its hazards: the temptation to smugness, self-satisfaction, and the easy condemnation of those who do not agree with us. But there is also, as Thessalonians reminds us, the potential for genuine suffering in acknowledging that one is an "insider" to some tradition. And there is also, as Matthew and Micah remind us, a stringent standard of behavior demanded of those who draw boundaries between insiders and outsiders. Our polemic against those outside must constantly be turned on ourselves. One might wonder at times if our contemporary exaltation of the outsider status might have less to do with humility and tolerance than it does with the avoidance of suffering and the flight from moral responsibility.

Twenty-fifth Sunday after Pentecost

Lutheran	Roman Catholic	Episcopal	Common Lectionary
Hos. 11:1-4, 8-9	Wisd. of Sol. 6:12-16	Amos 5:18-24	Amos 5:18-24
1 Thess. 5:1-11	1 Thess. 4:13-18	1 Thess. 4:13-18	1 Thess. 4:13-18
Matt. 25:14-30	Matt. 25:1-13	Matt. 25:1-13	Matt. 25:1-13

THE DAY OF THE LORD

What is it we expect of the future, or await from God? The theme of eschatology begins to be sounded as each liturgical year approaches the season of Advent. The conviction that history is tending toward a meaningful conclusion, that we await a culmination of God's work in history, is deeply rooted in our Christian tradition. But it is not necessarily a lively element in the faith of all Christians. Indeed, Christians today are perhaps more deeply divided on the issue of eschatology than on any other point of doctrine. Some millenarian Christians virtually define themselves in terms of an avid anticipation of the rapture. But other Christians (including probably those using the common lectionary) regard traditional expectation for the "day of the Lord" as an embarrassing reminder of a mythic structure of belief best left behind, or at best a symbol of the search for a new age that is the result of human social effort.

The readings lead us through the birth of eschatological expectation in Amos, its parabolic expression in Matthew, and its reinterpretation in Paul. We are invited to locate within our own life of faith the diverse moments of anticipation of which they speak. At a more fundamental level, we are challenged to consider whether any of this language makes sense to us.

FIRST LESSON: AMOS 5:18-24
THE DAY OF DARKNESS

The eighth century prophet Amos may have been the first to employ the term "day of the Lord" as an eschatological designation (For others, see Isa. 2:12; 13:6; Jer. 46:10; Zeph. 1:7, 14, 18; 2:3), but it is obvious from the form of this oracle that he was controverting an already popular belief. Less certain is the content of the earlier understanding. It seems to have involved Israel's positive expectation of help from Yahweh against its enemies (compare Jer. 46:10). Less certain is the connection of this expectation to the punctilious performance of sacrifices to Yahweh.

Prophetic books are literarily too complex for us to be overconfident in such matters. It is possible that oracles directed to separate situations might later have

43

been stitched together editorially. But if we read the text in its present arrangement, it is appropriate to note that the connection between ritual performance and confident expectation is at the very least implied: The oracle against external worship (5:21-24) follows immediately upon that concerning the day of the Lord (5:18-20), and can be read as providing the basis for the people's confidence in that day. According to this logic, Yahweh is their patron God, bound to them by a covenant of loyalty; their part of the bargain is kept by the offering of appropriate worship to Yahweh in preference to any other god; Yahweh, in turn, must keep his side of the deal by helping Israel to victory over its enemies.

Amos is the paradigmatic prophet of the Lord who resists the reduction of the covenant to ritual observance or magical security. He speaks in behalf of the Lord "whose name is the God of Hosts" (5:27), not some local suzerain whose patronage can be purchased with a payoff. Amos's thundering denunciation of such perversion retains freshness and power, for it addresses not only the distortions of ancient Israelite religion, but also the corruption implicit in every religious impulse seeking by human effort in the present to gain some predictable leverage on the future.

Amos's first surprise is reversing the terms of the people's expectation. They had thought of the "day of Yahweh" as a talisman of protection against their enemies, a day of blessing filled with "light" and "brightness" (5:18, 20). This oracle instead occurs within a series of threats addressed not against the nations, but against the "house of Israel" (5:1). The day they had expected to be "darkness" for their enemies and "light" for themselves will, says Amos, be exactly the opposite. It will not be a blessing but a woe (5:18). It will be "darkness" and "gloom," rather than the light and brightness they had anticipated (5:18, 20). The symbols of light and darkness are so basic and pervasive that we cannot be sure whether Amos was making allusion to the creation story, or to the Exodus experience. It is obvious, however, that the symbol of light is here associated with the powerful presence of the Lord, and darkness with his absence.

The straightforward threat of reversal is accompanied by a pair of striking analogies. They add to the threat a terrifying note of uncertainty. The day of the Lord will be like the case of a person who escaped from a lion, but then encountered a bear! Or like one who leaned against a wall and was bitten by a serpent (5:19)! In our ears there is something almost repelling in the random violence implied by these images, especially when it is clear that the *active* agent of hostility in each case is meant to refer to Yahweh, of whose help and assistance they were so certain. Yahweh is the bear that meets them, and the serpent coiled by the wall waiting to strike them!

Amos gives the reason for the reversal in the next oracle. The prophet declares in the name of Yahweh, "I hate, I despise your festivals . . . your solemn assemblies . . . I will not accept them" (5:21-22). Do we find here a protest against the use of ritual in religion? Far more likely, Amos is attacking the magical use of ritual, the performance of sacrifices and feasts to manipulate God. The prophet tells them that they have misplaced their efforts just as they have misplaced their confidence.

The covenant with Yahweh could not be satisfied by the making of cereal or animal sacrifices. The covenant of loyalty and love demanded the commitment of the human heart and mind and soul to the service of Yahweh. That commitment in turn was spelled out by the ethical demands of the law, expressed in the shorthand, "justice and righteousness."

In his earlier oracles against Israel, Amos charged that they abandoned Yahweh not only by worshiping at Bethel and Gilgal (5:5) but above all by their oppression of the poor (5:11), their taking of bribes, and their practice of injustice (5:12). It will now do them no good to turn to Yahweh with ritual observance. In order to fulfill their covenantal obligations, they must "let justice roll down like waters, and righteousness like an everflowing stream" (5:24). Otherwise, as the oracle continues, the day they expect as one of deliverance will turn out just the opposite. They will suffer defeat at the hands of their enemies and be taken in exile (5:27), not because Yahweh is powerless, but because he will not be mocked: "*I* will take you into exile' . . . says the LORD whose name is the God of hosts."

The prophet asserts the absolute sovereignty of the living God. Humans neither control history nor manipulate the Master of history. Their attempts to secure their own future by bribing God are doomed to failure, leading eventually to their own destruction. The prophet insists as well that the covenantal blessings cannot be purchased by means of religious observances, but are given as the gift of love in response to the human attitudes of loyalty and love toward the Lord. Finally, human loyalty toward the Lord is necessarily spelled out in dispositions of justice and righteousness toward the neighbor.

When we now read Amos, his statements about the day of Yahweh do not have the effect of focusing us on the future. Just the opposite: They point us to consider the present disposition of our hearts. Whether the day of the Lord is to be a blessing or woe does depend on us: not on our cultic actions but on our moral actions, not in our performance of worship but in our doing of justice. In this perspective, every day of covenantal fidelity can be designated as a day of the Lord, filled with the light and brightness of blessing.

GOSPEL: MATTHEW 25:1-13
A NIGHT OF SURPRISE

(For Matt. 25:14-30, see the Twenty-sixth Sunday after Pentecost.)

The parable of the wise and foolish virgins (Matt. 25:1-13) is unique to Matthew's Gospel. It appears in the middle of Jesus' lengthy eschatological discourse (24:1—25:46) delivered to his closest followers (and by implication to Matthew's readers) on the Mount of Olives while he was facing the temple grounds (24:1-3) after his final battle with the Pharisees and scribes (23:1-39). That last confrontation had concluded with the words, "You will not see me again until you say, 'Blessed is the one who comes in the name of the Lord' " (23:39). Since in Matthew's narrative that acclamation had already been made by Jesus' disciples (21:9), the reiteration naturally prompts a question concerning this new declaration, namely "the sign of your coming and the end of the age" (24:3).

Typical of Matthew's editing procedure, Jesus' response becomes a fully developed discourse dealing with the various stages that lead to the final establishment of "the kingdom of heaven" (25:1). The first section of the discourse is thoroughly apocalyptic in character, drawing from and adapting Mark 13. In his interpretation of Mark, Matthew expands the parenetic character of the discourse. He takes from Mark 13:32 the remarkable disclaimer concerning the *time* of the end: "But about that day and hour no one knows, neither the angels of heaven, nor the Son, but only the father" (Matt. 24:36). And on the basis of that indeterminacy, he develops the theme of watching and readiness.

That theme is developed with several analogies. There is a comparison to the days of Noah, when people were surprised by the flood in the midst of their everyday activities (24:37-40). In another, the owner of a house is surprised by the thief in the middle of the night (24:43). And finally, watching and readiness are advised for a household slave who fell to beating his underlings during the time of his master's delay but was surprised by the arrival of his master "on a day when he does not expect him and at an hour that he does not know," leading to his punishment (24:45-50). These examples serve as parabolic reminders of the situation of those awaiting the return of the Son of Man: "Watch therefore, for you do not know on what day your Lord is coming (24:42) . . . therefore you must also be ready, for the Son of Man is coming at an hour you do not expect" (24:44). That the parable of the virgins awaiting the bridegroom continues this same eschatological theme of readiness is made obvious by the narrator's conclusion, "Keep awake therefore, for you know neither the day nor the hour" (25:13).

The image of the bridegroom automatically evokes the prophetic image of the covenantal relationship between Yahweh and Israel in terms of a marriage (Hos. 2:14-23; Isa. 62:5; see Song of Sol. 4:8). Jesus may well have used the designation with reference to himself in a provocative saying preserved by all three Synoptic Gospels, "The wedding guests cannot fast while the bridegroom is with them, can they? As long as they have the bridegroom with them they cannot fast. The days will come when the bridegroom is taken away from them, and then they will fast on that day" (Mark 2:19-20; Matt. 9:14-17; Luke 5:33-38). We also find an implied appropriation of the image at the end of the book of Revelation, applied to Jesus and his return: "The Spirit and the bride say, 'Come!'" (Rev. 22:17).

Whatever Jesus intended by this parable, Matthew's readers would inevitably view it from a postresurrection perspective in terms of the expected return of Jesus as Son of Man. Thus, the manuscripts that omit "and the bride" (25:1) are certainly to be preferred, for it is the return of Jesus and not of a married couple that is here being imagined. Likewise, we recognize the designation of the bridegroom as "Lord" in 25:11 as referring to the resurrected Jesus (compare 20:8; 21:3; 21:40; 24:42; 25:19; 25:37), and the "delay" of the bridegroom (25:5) as a reference to the time before the return of the Son of Man (compare 24:48; 25:19). Both in imagery and structure, therefore, the parable has some striking similarities to the Matthean parable of the wedding feast (22:1-14).

The point of the parable is transparent, particularly when cast into the sapiential categories of "wisdom" and "foolishness" (25:2), for in the ancient world these characterizations referred above all to practical knowledge appropriately expressed. The virgins who were excluded from the marriage feast were foolish because they had not acted properly during the time of waiting: They had assumed the time would be short and their supplies sufficient. They neglected to perform either at the beginning or during the time of delay the tasks that would ensure their ability to perform their job. We can assume it was their assigned role to provide lighting for the entry of the married couple into the city. Their failure to prepare meant that they had failed to keep their implied covenant with the bridegroom. That their neglect reveals a more fundamental betrayal causes his stern rejection of them from the wedding party: "Truly I say to you, I do not know you" (25:12). The occasion that should have been light turned out to be for them in the most literal sense darkness. The door to the well-lighted banquet hall was closed, leaving them standing outside with no lights at all (25:11).

The virgins who greeted the bridegroom with lighted lamps and entered with him into the happy celebration were correspondingly wise because of their prudential action in preparing for a long delay and bringing with their lamps a sufficient supply of fuel. They took their covenant with the bridegroom seriously. They were ready to serve him when he arrived. The place they entered was for them light precisely because they brought with them their lamps.

Like the prophet Amos, Matthew turns the expectation for the day of the Lord into a warning. Language about the end again functions to focus attention on present attitudes and behavior. Because we do not know when the end is, we must always be ready. The time of waiting is not one for presumptuously sleeping until the bridegroom arrives. It requires of us the things demanded by covenant, so that we are prepared for his arrival.

SECOND LESSON: 1 THESSALONIANS 4:13-18
A DAY OF HOPE

(For 1 Thess. 5:1-11, see the Twenty-sixth Sunday after Pentecost.)

The prophetic and gospel texts addressed an attitude of complacency toward the day of the Lord. Paul's task, in contrast, is to arouse the Thessalonians from the lethargy of despair based in their perception that those who had died had no future. (1 Thess. 4:13-18). Paul had himself couched the good news to this community in eschatological terms. Their conversion was from idols to the service of the living and true God, "to wait for his Son from heaven, whom he raised from the dead—Jesus, who rescues us from the wrath to come" (1:9-10). In the meantime, individuals from the community have died, and members of the church are grieving them not only because of their human loss, but because they have decided that the deceased will miss out on God's triumph in history.

Paul takes their confusion sufficiently seriously to provide an elaborate response. We read only the first part in this lectionary passage. In the section that continues in next Sunday's reading, Paul makes the turn that we have found also in Amos and Matthew. He insists that God's ways are not controllable, and the time of the end is uncertain. He tries to focus the community's attention on their ethical behavior in the present (1 Thess. 5:1-11). But in the present section he provides an imaginative scenario of the end time, so that his readers could "encourage one another with these words" (4:13). Paul was no more in a position to know the exact stages of the end time than we are. Indeed, his letters actually contain several versions that are not entirely harmonious. The scenario sketched here is obviously dependent on apocalyptic imagery: the descent from heaven, the cry of command, the archangels' call, and the blast of the trumpet of God. Then, the gathering both of the dead and of the living into the clouds and into the presence of the Lord "so we will be with the Lord forever" (4:16-17).

Of greater importance than the details are the basic points Paul was trying to make by means of this imaginative portrayal. First, Paul considers their despair as a threat to their identity as Christians. They are acting "as others do who have no hope" (4:13). He means those who continue to worship the dead "idols" rather than the "living God" (1:9). The Thessalonians are in danger of slipping back into the perception of God as a limited and manipulable power rather than the very source of all reality. Second, Paul corrects their confusion by reminding them of the basis of their hope in this living God. As he had intimated in 1:10, this is the God who raised Jesus from the dead. The resurrection of Jesus is proof that the one with whom they have to do is the Creator who calls into being that which is not. Certainly, therefore, this God can give life back to those whose human life has ended: "Since we believe that Jesus died and rose again, even so, through Jesus, God will bring with him those who have died" (4:14). Why is losing sight of this to lose their identity? Because the resurrection of Jesus is the very basis of the community's existence in the first place. Finally, Paul asserts that all humans, whether alive or dead, are equal in the eyes of God, for whom all reality is immediately and equally present. Paul invokes an otherwise unknown word of the Lord to assure them of this fact: "We who are alive, who are left until the coming of the Lord, will by no means precede those who have died" (4:15).

Paul wants the Thessalonians to be comforted, not by a fairy tale about the future, but by the true basis of their hope in the power of the living God. He has created them; by the resurrection of Jesus he has saved them; and by the sending of the Spirit he sanctifies them (4:3). Their despair has paralyzed them from living out their faith and love. They need reminding that the day of the Lord *can* be brightness and light for those who place their hope in the living God who raised Jesus from the dead (1:10).

DO WE AWAIT AT ALL?

All three readings reflect the conviction that God's power is real and that God's interactions with the world are both real and decisive. The prophet warns those who rely smugly on their formal allegiance with this God to the neglect of their moral responsibilities. The gospel warns those who grow so weary and negligent in their waiting that they fall asleep and fail to make preparations for a coming that is certain, if delayed. Paul rouses to new hope those who have their conviction in a living and life-giving God threatened by the death of their loved ones.

We who now read these texts are certainly nearer the position of the Thessalonians than of the Israelites, with the difference that our doubts are increasingly conceptual as well as existential. It is true that many contemporary Christians still obsess over the near arrival of the parousia. But many more Christians, deeply infected by the germ of modernity, find the very idea of a future coming of the Lord to be incomprehensible. They either abandon the notion as one among other mythic elements of Christianity they have had to abandon, or they transmute it into a secular version of social action or liberation theology.

But if these texts represent an ineradicable part of our tradition, they challenge us to reconsider the stand that some of us may all too casually assume. Is it a faithful and careful response to such passages to declare (as I have been known to do), "All eschatological language serves a parenetic function; future talk focuses us on the present," if such a conclusion implicitly dismisses the content of such eschatological language? Is it possible to blithely reject the notion of God's day of visitation without fundamentally breaking with the continuum of "living God/resurrection/second coming" that Paul insists on in 1 Thessalonians?

Are those of us who bracket the eschatological terms of our theological lexicon not actually guilty in reverse of the same misapprehension usually attributed to millenarians? They, we declare, are obsessed with the *how* and *when* of the end time. They seek to disengage from the symbols of Scripture a schedule of events. But is it not our own inability to imagine the *how* or the *why* of God's final intervention that also leads us to dismiss the *reality* of that visitation, and reduce the Scriptures that speak of it only to the symbolic? If millenarians turn apocalyptic expectation into a conservative or reactionary social agenda, do we who invoke lightly baptized eschatological categories to adorn our liberal or radical social agendas make the same error? Such hard questions may not derive directly from any of these texts. But they surely are ones we must accept into our preaching if we are to hear them responsibly.

Twenty-sixth Sunday after Pentecost

Lutheran	Roman Catholic	Episcopal	Common Lectionary
Mal. 2:1-2, 4-10	Prov. 31:10-13, 19-20, 30-31	Zeph. 1:7, 12-18	Zeph. 1:7, 12-18
1 Thess. 2:8-13	1 Thess. 5:1-6	1 Thess. 5:1-10	1 Thess. 5:1-11
Matt. 23:1-12	Matt. 25:14-30	Matt. 25:14-15, 19-29	Matt. 25:14-30

THE QUALITY OF OUR WAITING

The readings for this Sunday also deal with the future day of the Lord. They express the expectation rooted in our tradition that God's business with us is by no means yet finished, that we await still another and more powerful encounter with God's presence, and that the character of that encounter is conditioned by the quality of our waiting for it. Working through last week's texts, we came to recognize that this element of the tradition is no longer obvious to all of us. Many of us in fact simply no longer believe in a future meeting between ourselves and God.

I suggested in the reflection on last Sunday's readings that our loss of eschatological expectation may be connected to a more fundamental collapse within the structure of our Christian faith. If we believe in a living God who creates the world and us anew at every moment, and who has raised Jesus from the dead to be present to us in the Spirit, what should shock us about the possibility of a further encounter? But if our belief is constrained by the limits of enlightenment rationality, even the concept of the "living God" appears mythical, and the hope for a future "coming" of God only a further mystification of the delusion.

In matters of eschatology, the distance between the symbolic world of the Scripture and the one inhabited by us is clear. But the texts will not go away. Nor can we dismiss them as marginal to the tradition. They are more central to the tradition than we are. The contemporary reader is therefore forced to make an unusually sharp decision: The texts should be abandoned because they are meaningless and scandalous; our contemporary ethos should be adjusted to conformity with our sacred texts; or, we must find a way to negotiate the space between these ancient symbols and ourselves without destroying either them or us. Before we decide to drink, desist, or dilute, it might be useful first to assess the strength of the broth over which we deliberate.

FIRST LESSON: ZEPHANIAH 1:7, 12-18
THE GREAT DAY IS A DAY OF WRATH

Even readers generally skeptical of eschatology cannot fail to be impressed by the grandeur of Zephaniah's vision. He opens his prophecy with the bald declaration, "I will utterly sweep away everything from the face of the earth, says the LORD" (1:2). The catastrophe will be cosmic in scope. But why? Has the earth itself somehow betrayed the Lord? No. The prophet's next oracle clarifies: "I will make the wicked stumble. I will cut off humanity from the face of the earth" (1:3). Whom does the prophet mean? "Those who have turned back from following the LORD, who have not sought the LORD or inquired of him" (1:6). All of these statements precede our lectionary passage. They alert us to the fact that in Zephaniah's vision, the day of the Lord—like that of his predecessor Amos—is not cheerful. But it also makes clear that the day of the Lord is a response to a crisis generated not by God, but by the behavior of humans on the earth.

The lectionary passage itself is dominated by eschatological language. Within a short passage, some variant of the term *day of the Lord* occurs twelve times. The prophet's vision furthermore is one of unmitigated gloom. The day of the Lord is one of punishment (1:8, 9, 12) and distress (1:15, 17), experienced as an outpouring of God's "wrath" (1:15). The punishment is directed against those who have "sinned against the LORD" (1:17), including "the officials and the king's sons" (1:8).

The targets for punishment are those who have sinned by their fraud and oppression against the neighbor: "all who leap over the threshold, and who fill their master's house with violence and fraud" (1:9). They are people who have relied on their wealth to protect them. But it cannot do so against God's punishment: "Neither their silver nor their gold will be able to deliver them on the day of the LORD's wrath" (1:18). The prophet promises that "all the traders have perished; all who weigh out silver are cut off" (1:11). Nor will human political power protect them: even "the warrior cries aloud there" (1:14).

It should be of particular interest to us that the prophet has a special animus toward people who deny the possibility of God's intervention, "who say in their hearts, 'the LORD will not do good, nor will he do harm'" (1:12). They thereby reveal why they put their trust in position, power, and possessions: They have not "sought the LORD or inquired of him" (1:6). They have instead followed the logic of covetousness, using fraud and trickery to acquire sufficient possessions to make themselves safe and secure. They deny that God is in any fashion involved with the world of humans, making them free to exploit the world and their fellows in any manner they please. In effect, they are like those the psalmist designates as "fools" who say in their hearts "there is no God" (Ps. 14:1).

The prophet likens such false complacency based in a willful rejection of God's claim on the world to the boasting of drunkards. He commands them to cease such speech: "Be silent before the Lord GOD" (1:7). Then, in a wonderful image, Zephaniah pictures the Lord tracking them down through the mean streets: "At that time I will search Jerusalem with lamps, and I will punish the people who rest complacently on their dregs" (1:12). Such people in particular will have all their efforts stymied: *Their* goods will be plundered, and *their* houses laid waste. Though they build houses, they shall not inhabit them; though they plant vineyards, they shall not drink wine from them (1:13).

Yet here is the shocking thing: The terror of the day of wrath is not directed solely at these sinners. It will affect all humans. Just as the prophet opened his book with the statement that the Lord would sweep clean the earth, so also he concludes this passage: "In the fire of his passion the whole earth shall be consumed . . . a terrible end he will make of all the inhabitants of the earth" (1:18). Why should all the earth suffer for the sins of some? The very offensiveness of the proposition presents perhaps the best way for us to appropriate this text to our own lives.

Suppose we were to hear Zephaniah's attacks as directed at those of us now living in the "technologically advanced" Western world? Is it not precisely on the basis of our effective denial of God's claim on creation ("He will not/cannot do good or ill") that has brought the Earth to the brink of ecological doomsday? Have we not exploited the Earth without renewing it? Have we not oppressed other peoples and defrauded them of their own resources for the sake of our being safe and secure in our heedless consumerism? Hasn't the peddling of the gospel of consumerism to other peoples and lands led only to the loss of their own culture and to destruction by ours? Are we not in the position of the "officials and the king's sons" attacked by Zephaniah, whose predatory practices led to the "terrible end [that God] will make of all the inhabitants of the earth" (1:8, 18)?

Perhaps if we begin to think of the day of the Lord less as a visit from without and more like a visitation from within, we can appreciate how it applies to our present sense of doom with respect to our own future on planet Earth. But what the prophet would have us do is not simply to start recycling and finding alternative sources of energy, or even to examine our profligate and Earth-destroying life-style that has brought us to this dismal moment. The prophet would, I think, ask us to repent of the idolatrous self-seeking and denial of God that lies at the basis of all such ravaging of the planet. Such conversion might start with "silence before the Lord God," with the recognition that, as in the case of Zephaniah's indictment, the tragic end of all humanity can result from a treacherous betrayal by the few.

GOSPEL: MATTHEW 25:14-30
THE USE OF GOD'S GIFTS

(For Matt. 23:1-12, see the Twenty-fourth Sunday after Pentecost.)

What would happen if we were to approach Matthew's parable of the talents from the same ecological perspective? We would be able to retain the sharp edge of Matthew's emphasis on individual responsibility, but we would be able to shift its application from the way in which we use the "talents" given us by God, to the way in which we are all called to a stewardship of the Earth.

Luke's parallel parable of the pounds (Luke 19:11-27) places the motif of the use of possessions within the framework of a larger political story about a nobleman who got a kingdom. It serves as an allegorical interpretation of Luke's own narrative about Jesus. Matthew's version, in contrast, fits nicely in his larger eschatological discourse of 24:1—25:46. The tale of a master who went on "a journey" (25:14) and remained gone "a long time" (25:19) before returning and settling accounts with his servants has, in this setting, an obvious application to the situation of Christians who await the return of Jesus. Like the parables of the household slave (24:45-51) and of the wise and foolish bridesmaids (25:1-13), the lesson is straightforward: The time of waiting for a master's return must be spent profitably if there is to be a reward. The first of these three parables warned against misbehavior; the second warned against negligence; the third calls for courageous and creative action.

Typical of Matthew's parables is that the principle of judgment be both in-dividual and strict (cf. Matt. 13:18-23; 21:28-31; 22:1-14). The distribution of talents is according to "each one's ability," so that no one was expected to perform beyond capacity. The amounts of money, however, are huge. A talent is equivalent to 60 *mnas* (the money distributed in Luke's version), and five talents would be an amount of about thirty thousand denarii. To get a sense of the amount, consider that Luke considers five hundred denarii to represent a large debt (Luke 7:41-42). The servants, in other words, are entrusted with a substantial amount of wealth. And each is held strictly to account. The first servant went "at once" to trade (25:16). Such energy and determination gained a share in the "joy of [the] master" (25:21, 23). Since there is no discrimination made in the reward, we must assume that the point was not the amount earned, but how each servant performed according to ability.

The punishment of the third servant is equally consistent. He tries to defend his failure to do anything with the money but bury it in the ground (25:18) on the basis of his fear of his master's expectations: He perceived his master as a man "reaping where [he] did not sow, and gathering where [he] did not scatter seed" (25:24). But this excuse is turned back on him. Precisely because "he knew" what sort of expectation the master had, he was obliged to do more than return what he had been given. What he calls fear (25:25), the master designates as wickedness and laziness (25:26). He has simply not lived up to the covenant expectations between the master and servant. If he lacked the will or intelligence to do something more with the master's wealth than simply "consume it" (by burying it), he could at least have given it to others so that they could make it profitable (25:27). His punishment is the converse of the blessing given to the good servants: They shared in the master's joy; he is excluded from the master's presence and thrown into the "outer darkness" (25:30).

Now, how might the ecological perspective derived from Zephaniah help us read this text? The easiest way is by allowing the parable to function allegorically. If the Gospel writers had no difficulty with this sort of application of Jesus' parables (Matt. 13:18-23, 36-43), why should we? We can easily identify ourselves as those who have been entrusted with great wealth by the Lord until his return. Especially those of us who inhabit the economically developed nations of the West must constantly be aware of how we have been made stewards of unparalleled wealth. The wealth entrusted to us, however, has little to do with the "stuff" we use to reassure ourselves of our existence in ever greater piles of possessions. It is rather the resources of the Earth itself that remain always the Lord's. We can also easily perceive that such stewardship demands of us courageous and creative action.

But what is the appropriate action to take with such wealth? The parable would suggest that it should lead to actions that increase the wealth of the Master. Such a reading would at first appear to delight the heart of a capitalist! But we need to pay closer attention. In the parable, the wealth gained by trade never becomes the possession of the servants themselves. They are managers for the Master, expected to create more wealth for *him*, not for themselves! The reward for their creativity is a place in the Lord's presence.

To translate the parable allegorically to our own circumstances means to understand the demand for an increase in the Master's wealth as a mandate to deal creatively and productively with the Earth's resources. This entails enabling it to be God's creation, allowing it to yield greater fruit for all, and sharing that productivity with all. Such fruitfulness requires that we not only take from creation but above all give back to it. We must invest the energy and effort required to share creation with all creatures. The failure to do this is the equivalent of burying the talent in the ground. Out of fearfulness—fear for our own safety and security— we simply use up the resources, giving nothing to others, and turning nothing back to the Lord except the soiled and unproductive coin that is the emblem of our wickedness and laziness.

SECOND LESSON: 1 THESSALONIANS 5:1-11
STAYING AWAKE AND ATTENTIVE

(For 1 Thess. 2:8-13, see the Twenty-fourth Sunday after Pentecost.)

Paul's First Letter to the Thessalonians continues the theme of the day of the Lord. The passage 5:1-11 advances the discussion of the end time that Paul had begun in 4:13-18 as a response to the despair of community members who considered those recently dead to have missed out on God's triumphant establishment of his kingdom. Paul there provided the true ground of hope for the future, which is their faith in the living God who raised Jesus from the dead (4:14). Now Paul turns to the attitudes that should characterize their time of waiting.

He begins by warning that the day of the Lord will come without advance notice. They know well that it will come like a "thief in the night" (5:2). The image occurs in the Synoptic eschatological discourses as a warning to be attentive: "If the owner of the house had known in what part of the night the thief was coming, he would have stayed awake and would not have let his house be broken into. Therefore you also must be ready, for the Son of Man is coming at an unexpected hour" (Matt 24:43). Paul also uses the image of a woman in labor, capturing both the inexorability of the event and the suddenness of its climax (5:3). The birth of a child is a positive thing. Paul uses the analogy, however, to warn against the onset of "sudden destruction" that comes upon them. This is the first hint in Paul's present discussion that he has in his mind the traditional understanding of the day of the Lord as a day of punishment for sinners. That this is the background for his exhortation is shown by his reassurance in 5:9, "God has destined us not for wrath," a statement which echoes the "day of wrath" from Zeph. 1:15 as well as Paul's own kerygmatic statement concerning "Jesus, who rescues us from the wrath that is coming" (1 Thess. 1:10).

The destruction is destined to fall first on those who depend on everything continuing just the way it always has. They are the spiritual heirs of Zephaniah's skeptics, who insisted that "The LORD will not do good, nor will he do harm" (Zeph 1:12). They effectively deny God's claim on the world. Paul characterizes them as saying "There is peace and security" (1 Thess. 5:3). The Greek reads almost like a mantra ("peace and security") recited by those denying the doom that impends because of their vice and neglect.

Paul insists that his readers are not among this group, but his reminder has the effect of an exhortation: "Do not be among this group." They are to be a community not of darkness but of light, "children of the light and children of the day." The language resembles the self-designation used by the Jewish sectarians at Qumran. But Paul does not use the epithet as an excuse for smugness. Rather, he demands that the community demonstrate the characteristics of those who live in the day and inhabit the light.

Nighttime people are like those resting "on their lees" in Zeph. 1:12. They hang out in bars getting drunk and boasting of their invulnerability. Then they fall into the sodden sleep of the narcotized: "Those who sleep sleep at night, and those who get drunk get drunk at night" (5:7). But Paul insists that the Thessalonians are not to act in this way: "Let us not fall asleep as others do, but let us keep awake and be sober" (5:6), and he repeats in 5:8, "But since we belong to the day, let us be sober."

Paul calls the community to an eschatological attentiveness. The approaching end time is certain because ours is a living God who will make his claim on creation. Humans have no choice in that matter. But they do have a choice concerning the quality of their waiting for that day. They can hide from the reality and pretend that their inability to figure out how it will happen means it won't happen. They can treat their lives as though all that mattered was the peace and security of the moment. But to act that way is to be a child of the night who gets drunk and then sleeps it off.

The Christian community is called to an active engagement with the future. The Thessalonians are to be like soldiers who have been wakened at dawn by reveille to put on armor for battle. Their attentiveness is not to be an obsessive worrying over timetables and schedules. Neither is it to be passive handwringing over the inevitable collapse of all things. It is rather to decisively act out their identity in the world: "Put on the breastplate of faith and love, and for a helmet the hope of salvation" (5:8). Paul assures them that they are not destined to be victims of the wrath to come. They will obtain "salvation through our Lord Jesus Christ" (5:9).

In hope of that victory, they can do battle against the forces of lethargy and evil. Whether as individuals they survive or die is not the issue. Their hope is not rooted in the survival of their bodies, or of their children, or even of the planet. Their hope is rooted in the living God whose ability to renew life is demonstrated in the resurrection of Jesus, "who died for us, so that whether we wake or sleep we might live with him" (5:10). The issue, rather, is obedient faith in the God who creates the world anew every morning!

Can Paul's eschatological exhortation carry anything of the ecological dimension we have detected in Zephaniah and Matthew? At first glance, the possibility seems slight. Paul's assurance that his readers will be carried up on the clouds to be with Jesus (4:17), and that they are not destined for wrath but for salvation (5:9) seems to feed directly into millenarian speculations about the rapture of the saints preceding the great tribulation. As we have seen, that sort of eschatological fixation tends to exclude any ecological awareness. In some versions, it seems almost as if this earth that is God's creation were simply a disposable package, ready for the dump once emptied of its precious cargo of souls. Even more shockingly, televangelists wed such an expectation for the end time to a lightly baptized version of American consumerism. Material prosperity and consumption is identified as the blessing of God's elect during the time of waiting for removal.

To take Paul's reassurance that way is to miss his point entirely. He does not want his readers to sit on their hands and stop their daily activities. He does not want them to withdraw from the world and wait for the Lord. And he certainly does not want them to act like sleepers and drunkards, who continue to live as though the end were not coming. The alertness he calls for is an attentiveness to the demands of their life before God. It would be unthinkable for Paul to consider obedient faith in the Creator as compatible with the destruction of the Earth. Faith in God and the care for God's creation are inseparable. When Paul concludes this passage with the exhortation that they should "encourage one another and build up each other, as indeed you are doing" (5:11), he does not have in mind simply the reassurance about the future of those who have died; he has in mind particularly the present behavior of those who are still alive.

THE QUALITY OF OUR WAITING

Despite the distance from our consciousness of any traditional expectation of the end time, the texts speak of that future encounter with the Lord in terms of unequivocal conviction. They do not waste time on the *how* or *when* of the event. They focus instead on the quality of our time of waiting for it. Perhaps here we can begin to find ways of making these texts speak to our own experience. In fact, we do face an encounter with an end to our lives as we know them. An end of our planet is not inconceivable, and it is directly linked to the patterns of material consumption rooted in our effective denial of God as Creator.

These passages suggest that something more is required of us than the attempt to forestall disaster. Yes, we should conserve and protect and recycle and develop alternative sources of energy. But these in themselves do not constitute a response of faith. They may only be a sign of fear. Our tradition calls us to the response of faith that demands a constant conversion of obedience to God and God's claims on the world.

The quality of our waiting is in large measure shaped by the ways in which we as a community form a consciousness of who we are and what we are called to. We can encourage each other to be "sleepers and drunkards" who deny the presence of God and continue to lay waste the world. Or we can be a community that builds a shared identity of care for creation, a community that lives out, and thereby exemplifies for others an alternative view of the world and its origin and destiny.

Christ the King
Last Sunday after Pentecost

Lutheran	Roman Catholic	Episcopal	Common Lectionary
Ezek. 34:11-16, 23-24	Ezek. 34:11-12, 15-17	Ezek. 34:11-17	Ezek. 34:11-16, 20-24
1 Cor. 15:20-28	1 Cor. 15:20-26, 28	1 Cor. 15:20-28	1 Cor. 15:20-28
Matt. 25:31-46	Matt. 25:31-46	Matt. 25:31-46	Matt. 25:31-46

THE KING OF LOVE MY SHEPHERD IS

At least half the fun in being Christian is seeing how many paradoxes we can carry without collapsing. The readings of the preceding Sundays made us struggle with the notion that God involves himself with the world at all. On top of that we tossed the absurd conviction that God will intervene in our history in a climactic judgment. Wobbling under these cumbrous packages, we stagger to the final Sunday after Pentecost, only to discover that we must add to our stack of puzzlers this final and perhaps most dubious one: that the reign of God in history is established through a human being who died as a criminal.

A gap greater than a chasm separates our everyday world of work, and the world we enter when we read these texts. To declare within our increasingly closed circuited and hominized universe that there is a God at all constitutes a shocking proposition. To insist that God rules the world and calls it to account is more provocative still. And to declare that this rule is exercised through a crucified Messiah whom we call King is an excess of paradox. Walking from our profane and everyday world—especially in America where the very *concept* of kingship is by definition unpatriotic—into the church to hear these readings is at the very least a declaration of allegiance to another and more richly humorous understanding of the world.

The problem of course is that we do experience these declarations only as paradoxes. They are affirmations that seem to contradict the experiences and convictions by which we ordinarily live. Yet we keep coming back to hear them. Does it not worry us that we listen week after week to statements that we scarcely understand and if we did probably would not really believe? Why do we induce such psychic dissonance into our lives? Why don't we allow ourselves to sink pleasantly into the narcotized world around us that insists there is no God, no rule of God, no coming judgment, and certainly no messianic King?

Can it be because we recognize, however dimly, that without the measure of absurdity offered us by these texts our lives would be more boring and filled with quiet despair? Can it be that part of the freedom offered us by our faith is that freedom of play that is pretending, and that without such play there is only grim labor? Can it be that some still alive part of us knows that only in a kingdom can one truly play, and that only in God's kingdom is freedom fun?

FIRST LESSON: EZEKIEL 34:11-24
THE KING AS SHEPHERD

The image of the king as shepherd was deeply rooted in the ideology of the ancient Near East. But in obvious ways it is an image that offends our contemporary sensibilities. It suggests a relationship between executive and governed that does not derive from the will of the governed (the sheep are not consulted nor do they elect their shepherd) but on the intelligence and will of the executive. It thereby implies further that an executive knows better than the flock where it should pasture and how it might survive attacks of predators. But why do we dislike the image, or even the very idea of kings?

Our antipathy derives in part from the enlightenment conviction that the good of the individual is more important than the good of the group. We therefore resist the notion of being defined as a "flock." As part of that philosophically derived individualism, we operate with the premise that each one of us is a king with respect to one's own life. We therefore resist the tyranny of any group's demands over us. Since such demands can never be so efficiently or directly enunciated as by an individual executive, the very notion of a king is distasteful. When it is joined to the image of the shepherd guiding a passive and stupid flock of sheep, we are even more insulted. We do not like being governed generally, and by an individual who is perceived as superior in particular. Our experience of kings has also suggested that if they have no one controlling them they are less likely to care for the flock than to their own needs, and may even sacrifice the people for the sake of their own ambitions.

In fact such abuse of authority has generated the prophet's attack on the kings of Israel as bad shepherds of the sheep. Instead of caring for the people, they have been concerned only for themselves (34:2). He lists the ways in which they have failed the sheep: They have not strengthened the weak, healed the sick, bound up the crippled, brought back those that strayed, or sought out the lost (34:4). Instead, they have exploited the sheep, gathering wealth from them but showing them no care. Instead, "with force and harshness you have ruled them" (34:4). As a result, the people/flock has been devastated and scattered, because "the shepherds have fed themselves, and have not fed my sheep" (34:8). The prophet is convinced that the experience of disaster and loss issuing in the Exile was to be blamed in large measure on the failed leadership of Israel's kings.

Attacks against tyranny make sense to Americans. They are built into the ideological justification for our democracy. They sound especially pertinent in a period when even elected politicians are viewed ever more negatively as acquisitive and corrupt, serving their own careers rather than the people. The difficulty for us today, however, is that we have no real standard against which to hold our petty tyrants. If we insist that our leaders be no greater than us, and if we are ourselves thoroughly self-serving in our individualism, where can we turn for assistance from these only slightly-larger-than-life-size mirrors of our own morality?

If their corruption is accompanied by administrative ineptitude we may grow angry enough to choose a strong-arm tyrant who can serve our passions more efficiently. The precedents are frightening even within our lifetime. But neither elected tyrants nor tyrannical electors can appeal to an image of shepherding larger and more gracious than that of barnyard management.

But the reality of just such an alternative model is what gave force to Ezekiel's charge against the kings of Israel. If they were appointed by the Lord to shepherd the people, then they were called to match the Lord's standard of care. Their kingship was to be defined not in terms of how long they could rule, or how many nations they could conquer, or how much profit they could turn from the wool trade, but simply in terms of the good of the flock! To be a king meant not to oppress the flock but to spend one's life for it in care, concern, and protection. The true shepherd would not seek to gain food from the flock so much as to feed it; to clothe himself from its produce so much as keep it warm and sheltered; to risk its existence for the sake of his comfort so much as to exhaust his own resources for the sake of its existence.

Ezekiel promises that if human rulers fail to live up to these standards, then the Lord himself would assume the role of shepherd, doing all the things that their human rulers had not: seeking them out and rescuing them when they were lost (34:12); feeding them in good places (34:13-14); healing the sick and binding up the crippled (34:16): "I myself will be the shepherd of my sheep . . . I will feed them with justice" (34:15-16). The flock that is the people has in the rule of God some recourse from human tyranny. In fact, the prophet declares, God will intervene by appointing a human shepherd to represent him and be the sort of king God desires: "he shall feed them and be their shepherd." The prophet identifies this shepherd as "my servant David" (34:23-24). But since David was by the time of Ezekiel already long dead, the oracle must concern one of David's descendants. Certainly that was the way the passage was understood as referring to the coming anointed One. Thus the first Christians recognized in the care and compassion of Jesus a proof that he was indeed the shepherd king promised by the Lord (see, e.g., Mark 6:34; Luke 15:3-7; John 10:11-18; 1 Pet. 2:25).

Ezekiel's message is by no means simply one of comfort. In the part of the passage that the lectionary inexplicably omits (34:17-22), the prophet also utters in the name of the Lord words of judgment directed at the flock itself: "As for you, my flock, thus says the Lord GOD" (34:17). The lectionary's omission of this section is all the more puzzling since they point most obviously toward the lectionary's own choice of a gospel passage: "I shall judge between sheep and sheep, rams and goats" (34:17). Ezekiel declares that the people themselves have a responsibility for their behavior, to which God holds them accountable.

If the king-shepherd's role toward them should be characterized by justice, so equally should their behavior toward each other. The principle of judgment therefore is one that applies to the people as well as the king. The prophet condemns those who not only feed on good pasture and drink clear water, but who "tread down with your feet the rest of your pasture," and in the water, "foul the rest with your feet" (34:18). He condemns those who "push with flank and shoulder, and butted at all the weak animals with your horns until you scattered them far and wide" (34:21). God therefore not only condemns the wicked shepherd and vows to rule the people himself with justice; God also condemns those sheep who act oppressively toward their fellows.

SECOND LESSON: 1 CORINTHIANS 15:20-28
MESSIANIC KINGDOM/GOD'S RULE

Although we recognize in Jesus' compassionate care for his people the sign of the authentic messianic Shepherd promised by Ezekiel, we confess that Jesus himself did not enter fully into kingly power until his resurrection. The conviction is expressed by the New Testament's frequent use of Ps. 110:1 with reference to the resurrection as Jesus' enthronement as God's Vicegerent: "The LORD said to my lord, 'Sit at my right hand until I make your enemies your footstool.'" That imagery is used by Paul in this lectionary reading from 1 Corinthians. The passage occurs in the middle of Paul's lengthy discussion of the resurrection. The reason Paul takes up the subject (one of only two in the letter not generated by specific reports or questions put to him by the community) is to provide the lively and not entirely stable Corinthians with the proper understanding of their place in God's kingdom. In the process, Paul also clarifies for us the place of Christ the King.

At least some of the Corinthian Christians seemed to have been convinced that because of the powerful gifts accompanying the bestowal of the Holy Spirit, they had entered God's eschatological kingdom, and already exercised authority within it. Paul notes their presumption with obvious sarcasm: "Already you have all you want! Already you have become rich! Quite apart from us you have become kings! Indeed, I wish that you had become kings, so that we might be kings with you" (4:8). The fantasy of already living in the end time also led them to neglect their moral behavior. They developed elitist attitudes toward others. They showed more concern with their own prestige than with the building up of the community (see 5:1-2; 6:7-8, 12-20; 8:11-12; 11:21-32). Paul's hope is that by showing them where they are in God's plan for the world, he may also instruct them in the proper behavior for their present time and place.

His argument proceeds in three stages. First Paul asserts that the kingship of Jesus consists in more than shepherding a specific people in a certain locality. By his resurrection Jesus enters into a cosmic rule. Jesus is not simply a Jewish Messiah. He is the new Adam who heads up a new creation in which "all will be made alive" (15:22). Christ is the "first fruits" of the life of which the Corinthians have been given a pledge by their reception of the Holy Spirit (15:23). Paul's way of understanding the kingship of Christ (which became the normative way of understanding it for Christians) involves an obvious reinterpretation of the terms of traditional Jewish messianic expectation. If the reign of God is not to be identified with the social structures of a specific population, but with God's rule over creation, the immediate lesson that follows is that the kingdom of God is not to be defined by traditional understandings of human power.

Paul next argues that the reign of Christ is itself temporary. As Ezekiel promised a human shepherd through whom God could rule the people, so is Jesus God's vicegerent in virtue of his resurrection. He will rule until, as the psalm has it, "he has put all his enemies under his feet" (15:25). These enemies include all the cosmic forces holding humans captive, designated as rules, authorities, and powers (15:24). The final and most intractable enemy is death itself (15:26). The resurrection of Jesus has begun that victory, but it will not be completed until all have been raised. Then the reign of Christ will end, when he "hands over the kingdom to God the Father" (15:24). When he has done that, even the Son will "be subjected to the one who put all things in subjection under him, so that God may be all in all" (15:28). The lesson the Corinthians are to derive is that if even Christ the King is subject to God, so must they; and that if the kingdom is still at battle with forces of evil, they can only participate in the rule of God by themselves joining that battle, first of all in their own lives.

The third part of Paul's argument continues after our lectionary passage. He drives home the moral imperative derived from this reality. The Corinthians who pride themselves on their spiritual prowess but neglect the most basic moral rules are deceiving themselves. Christ has risen, but they have not. In their fantasy resurrection kingdom, they resemble those who declare "Let us eat and drink, for tomorrow we die" (15:32). They are forgetting that *they* still must die and face judgment. Such heedless behavior represents a betrayal even of the experience of God that has been granted them: "For some people have no knowledge of God. I say this to your shame" (15:34).

GOSPEL: MATTHEW 25:31-46
THE FINAL JUDGMENT

The climax of Matthew's extensive eschatological discourse is reached in a final parable of the kingdom (25:31-46). The magnificent scene of final judgment carried out by Jesus contains elements of the shepherd image derived from Ezekiel: His act of judgment is depicted as a separation "as a shepherd separates the sheep from the goats" (25:32). As in the prophet, the flock is held to a standard of moral behavior (25:41-45).

But the parable bears even more unmistakable signs of the Christian reinterpretation of messiahship. The judgment is carried out by Jesus, after all, when he comes in his glory and sits "on the throne of his glory" (25:31; cf. 1 Cor. 15:23). The stakes are not simply temporal: Those worthy enter "eternal life" and those judged unworthy enter "eternal punishment" (25:46). And the judgment is made not only for Israel but for "all the nations"; it is cosmic in scope. Christ's judgment, furthermore, is one carried out in service to his Father: "The king will say to those at his right hand, 'Come, you that are blessed by my Father, inherit the kingdom prepared for you from the foundation of the world'" (23:34; see 1 Cor. 15:24-28).

The element most showing the effect of Christian reflection on the meaning of Christ's kingship is the standard of behavior that forms the basis of judgment. As in Matthew's other eschatological parables, people are held to account for their actions during that period of time when their master is away (see 24:45-51; 25:1-13, 14-30). But the actions now are not simply those of alert readiness, or prudential preparation, or the creative use of possessions. They are specified in terms of service to other humans, above all in providing real physical and spiritual assistance to those who are powerless and in distress. In the hungry, the thirsty, the stranger, the naked, and the imprisoned we catch an echo of Ezekiel's list of afflicted persons for whom the kings of Israel had failed to care (Ezek. 34:4). Those who have cared for such as these are rewarded with eternal life; those who have failed to care for such as these receive eternal punishment.

The most striking aspect of this standard, however, is that care for the needy is identified as service rendered to the king. Jesus tells those he rewards, "I was hungry and you gave me food" (25:35); likewise he tells those he punishes, "I was hungry and you gave me no food" (25:42). The parable's drama is supplied by the surprised (or plaintive) response from those so judged: "Lord, when was it that we saw you hungry and gave you food" (25:37, 44)? The king had been absent. How could they have been doing these things for him? The response, of course, is that this is the shepherd king promised by Ezekiel, who identifies himself completely with the sheep in his care, so that, "as you did it to one of the least of these who are members of my family, you did it to me" (25:40), and, even more frighteningly, "As you did not do it to one of the least of these, you did not do it to me" (25:45).

"WHY DO MEN THEN NOW NOT RECK HIS ROD?"

This line from Gerard Manley Hopkins's poem, "God's Grandeur" occurs almost naturally as we ponder these lessons. Ezekiel attacks the ways in which earthly kings seek their own advantage and neglect their people. But he also attacks the people for following exactly the same moral behavior of self-aggrandizement and oppression. He promises that God himself will shepherd the people through a descendant of David in a rule that fulfills the ideal of true shepherding.

Paul and Matthew find in Jesus the fulfillment of Ezekiel's promise. The fulfillment was not obvious, but paradoxical. How can we call a crucified criminal the king of anything? But the resurrection experience prompts us to look closer. In the death of Jesus we find the perfect expression of God's total identification with his people: As God's vicegerent, Jesus gave himself totally in service to others. He held nothing back. In the resurrection of Jesus, his kingly rule is initiated. It will not reach its completion until the spiritual forces binding humans are defeated. But in this meantime, those who "reck his rod" are held to the same standards of behavior toward each other that Jesus demonstrated toward them: They are not to live their lives for themselves but in service to each other. Indeed, so completely is Jesus identified with his members that what they do to each other for good or ill is in fact done to him. Such is the standard by which they will be judged.

In spelling things out so clearly, perhaps I have answered the question why we do not want to "reck his rod," that is, accept his kingship. It has little to do with our discomfort with the political implications of kingship, just as our disbelief in God's effective judgment has little to do with scientific judgments concerning the origin and destiny of the world. It has to do, rather, with the fact that we do not want to live under such a standard of behavior. One of the sad truths about democracy is that we have come to elect just the rulers we deserve: revolting from greatness or nobility of behavior in our own lives, we refuse to have as our leaders anyone who might challenge us to such behavior by exemplifying it.

By refusing to have Christ as our king, we can each sit as sovereigns on imaginary thrones. But such royalty is wearisome. We must always be insisting on service from others, just as they are insisting on obeisance from us. We must go to war to secure and protect our boundaries. We must accumulate wealth to ensure our security and embellish our dignity. How tedious. How boring. Can it really be that we never have fun, because we have no freedom, because we have no faith in God our king?